Overlay

Young Architects 16
Overlay

Foreword by Preston Scott Cohen
Introduction by Anne Rieselbach

Young & Ayata
The LADG
SIFT Studio
Norman Kelley
Jenny Sabin Studio
Geoffrey von Oeyen Design

Princeton Architectural Press
The Architectural League of New York

Published by
Princeton Architectural Press
37 East 7th Street
New York, New York 10003
www.papress.com

To view interviews with each firm, please
visit The Architectural League's website at
www.archleague.org.

Editor: Barbara Darko
Cover design: Pentagram
Interior layout: Mia Johnson

Special thanks to: Meredith Baber,
Nicola Bednarek Brower, Janet Behning,
Erin Cain, Megan Carey, Carina Cha,
Andrea Chlad, Tom Cho, Benjamin English,
Russell Fernandez, Jan Cigliano Hartman,
Jan Haux, Diane Levinson, Jennifer
Lippert, Katharine Myers, Jaime Nelson,
Rob Shaeffer, Sara Stemen, Marielle Suba,
Kaymar Thomas, Paul Wagner, Joseph
Weston, and Janet Wong of Princeton
Architectural Press
—Kevin C. Lippert, publisher

This publication is supported, in part, by
public funds from the New York City
Department of Cultural Affairs in partnership
with the City Council and the New York
State Council on the Arts with the support of
Governor Andrew Cuomo and the New York
State Legislature.

Installation photos at Parsons The New
School for Design © David Sundberg/Esto

Library of Congress
Cataloging-in-Publication Data

Young architects 16 : overlay / foreword by
Preston Scott Cohen ; introduction by Anne
Rieselbach. — First edition.
pages cm — (Young architects ; 16)
ISBN 978-1-61689-369-9 (pbk.)
1. Architectural League Prize for Young
Architects and Designers—Exhibitions.
2. Architecture—Awards—United States.
3. Architecture—United States—History--
21st century. 4. Young architects—United
States. I. Cohen, Preston Scott, writer
of foreword. II. Rieselbach, Anne, writer of
introduction. III.Architectural League of
New York.
NA2340.Y679956 2015
720.79'73--dc23
                                2014038612

Contents

The Architectural League of New York
Board of Directors 2014–2015

Acknowledgments

Each stage of the League Prize for Young Architects + Designers—from the competition to the presentations, installations, and subsequent publications—benefits from the support of the larger design community. The program begins with the work of the League Prize committee, a small group of past competition winners who draft the annual theme to address current issues in architectural design and theory. Entrants to the competition—open to North American residents who have been out of undergraduate or graduate school for ten years or less—submit a design portfolio and explanatory text in response to the theme, which for this thirty-third annual League Prize program was "Overlay."

Entries are reviewed by the committee members and prominent members of the design community. The League would like to thank committee members Ajmal Aqtash, Beat Schenk, and Bryan Young, as well as jurors Preston Scott Cohen, Evan Douglis, Florian Idenburg, Jennifer Lee, Charles Renfro, and Annabelle Selldorf. Their informed and discerning review resulted in an exceptional collection of work.

Competition winners are invited to create a site-specific installation of their work, present lectures, and publish their work in a catalog. They are the subjects of features on the League's website, archleague.org, which include interviews, slideshows, and video excerpts from their lectures. Michael Bierut and Britt Cobb of Pentagram once again designed a vibrant graphic identity for the program, from the call for entries to the installation graphics and the cover of this catalog, so ably produced by the team at Princeton Architectural Press. The catalog includes some of the many installation photographs generously shot by David Sundberg/ESTO. Thanks also to the Sheila C. Johnson Design Center at Parsons The New School for Design for cosponsoring the exhibition and lecture series, and the Johnson Design Center staff, Radhika Subramaniam, Kristina Kaufman, and Daisy Wong.

The League Prize program is made possible by the generous support of Dornbracht, Elise Jaffe + Jeffrey Brown, and Tischler und Sohn; by the Next Generation Fund of The Architectural League; and, in part, by public funds from the New York State Council on the Arts with the support of Governor Andrew Cuomo and the New York State Legislature and the New York City Department of Cultural Affairs in partnership with the City Council.

Foreword
Overlay: Authorship and Its Antinomies
Preston Scott Cohen

The Architectural League Prize for Young Architects + Designers invariably forecasts the future state of the art, the discipline, the academy, and the profession of architecture. The winners' work represents not only what has most recently influenced the best young people in the field but also how they are thinking about taking it forward in practices that deviate from the norm in order to break new ground.

This year, the winners responded to the theme "Overlay." Twenty years ago, when I was a prize recipient and the language of architecture was still very much on people's minds, the word would have evoked formal concepts, such as collage and montage—after all, we were living in the aftermath of postmodernism and deconstruction. But brewing in the background was a very different concern: the disparity, originating in the time of Walter Gropius, between the significance accorded to individual neo-avant-garde practitioners versus corporate firms. Today, the discussion about the relevance of the various modes of practice occupies the foreground.

The League is one of the most important cultural institutions that continue to support personally initiated forms of architectural authorship. Its League Prize Award valorizes alternatives to the usual career paths of young practitioners. The winning designers commit themselves to authoring exceptional types of projects as opposed to those of the established firms, whose employees are mandated to confront conventional and pervasive design tasks.

Interestingly, it turns out that the Overlay exhibition itself was overlaid on—that is, took place at the same time as—one of the most controversial renunciations of architectural authorship in recent memory: the 2014 Venice Architecture Biennale Exhibition titled Elements of Architecture, curated by Rem Koolhaas. In contrast to the League's collection of individual, speculative projects, which are exhibited in a manner similar to that of a typical Biennale, Elements was produced by an army of young architects under the intellectual mentorship of a single author.

Koolhaas proclaims the fundamental elements that constitute the core of contemporary architecture to be neither novel nor speculative. Rather, we inherit the elements—ramps, escalators, windows, balconies, walls, toilets, and so on—from the nineteenth and twentieth centuries. Koolhaas's exhibition texts read as dark and clever aphorisms that rehearse themes from his seminal texts such as

"Bigness," "Typical Plan," and "Junk Space." Though the Biennale texts are merely anecdotal and lack the narrative momentousness of the earlier writings, they are nonetheless provocative in the context of the Biennale, where they serve as "showstoppers" of sorts. Koolhaas, the curator, effectively grinds to a halt the culture producers' raison d'être. His catalog of elements supplants the Biennale's expected parade of spectacular (and sometimes surprising) new works and directions in architecture. The show instead offers only what is intractable, persistent, and normative in architecture.

Arguably, Koolhaas's historical approach to contemporaneity picks up where Paolo Portoghesi—the curator of The Presence of the Past, the first Venice Architecture Biennale Exhibition in 1980—left off, but there is a profound difference. Unlike his predecessor, Koolhaas exhibits no thirst for innovation and recommends no course of action. What we get is something more like a prognosis perhaps best exemplified by his text about a nineteenth-century invention: "The escalator is a particularly efficient symbol of the state of our global system, churning with continuous dynamism, offering the exact same thing everywhere, while haunted in its hidden guts by the suspicion that business as usual can't go on forever."

The contents of the Koolhaas exhibition represent the essence of what the League Prize winners resist. Yet, despite the apparent incommensurability between the two concurrent exhibitions, it is possible to discern parallel and dialectical relationships between Koolhaas's discourse and that of Overlay's group of exhibitors. Take, for example, Kutan Ayata and Michael Young, who are committed to experimentation and the production of novel forms through computational technologies; their stated ambition is to discover new organizational paradigms. This emphasis on program clearly establishes their work as an extension of the modern functionalist legacy and its suppression of formal motives, which has been relentlessly reinforced by Koolhaas. Similarly, the dual commitment of Claus Benjamin Freyinger and Andrew Holder of The LADG—to engage advanced design strategies and technologies in a lablike setting and then to export them for use in "real-world building," as they aptly put it—reveals their awareness of the two sides of the current architectural culture equation: willful innovation versus pragmatic capitulation.

Jenny Sabin dodges the bullets of the intractable elements altogether, opting to advance architecture by other means. Her exploration of biological models of growth and transformation is an unmistakable foil to the prevailing and dominant practice confined and dulled by the conventional elements of architecture. In this sense, her work illuminates the gap between the neo-avant-garde compulsion to valorize novelty as opposed to the multitude of more subtle forms of engagement manifest, to varying degrees, as entrenchment, intensification, or resistance.

The unusual manipulation of the cards dealt to architects, as opposed to the invention of new forms: this is the means by which the remaining three prizewinners—Adam Fure of SIFT Studio, Carrie Norman and Thomas Kelley, and Geoffrey von Oeyen—proceed to operate. Fure accepts the "ontology" of artifacts, with the assumption that the physical traits of things matter more than their willful composition according to any author's intention. Norman and Kelley adopt conventional and ordinary artifacts of culture and through distortion refer back to the Russian formalists' strategy of defamiliarization, imbuing lifeless objects with linguistic implications. Von Oeyen extracts heretofore invisible spatial properties from the conventional, typological substrate of buildings. Rather than start with the ambition to generate novelty, von Oeyen, like Koolhaas and his forbearer exhibitors in Portoghesi's Presence of the Past, prefers to discover new possibilities within the intractable givens, turning otherwise functionally necessary forms into optical devices that induce spatial experiences.

The opposition between those who seek to extend the avant-garde through authorship and those who wish to act as instruments who transform what is otherwise determined by forces beyond their control is perhaps among the most salient dialectics of the discipline in our time. It is for this reason that the work of the six recipients this year will provide a lasting and valuable testament.

Introduction

Anne Rieselbach, Program Director
The Architectural League of New York

This year's theme, "Overlay," explored how contemporary concepts of the term—iterative, conceptual, and notational—"drive discourse, tension between iterations, design solutions, and the parameters by which work is reviewed." The call for entries asked for work evidencing interpretations of overlay, "from process to presentation to product," that had the potential to define each firm's design identity.

In translating the work contained in their competition portfolios for the exhibition, competition winners expanded the ideas underlying their design processes with installations that explored possibilities for interpreting overlay, often by creating pieces that tested and expanded earlier work. The projects displayed—from graphic investigation to reimagined structural forms, material experimentation to intrinsic or applied patterns and finishes—examined how the design process might affect program as well as constructed form.

Carrie Norman and Thomas Kelley's installation, *Whitney's View*, literally drew on the theme with a graphic overlay referencing the iconic 1964 image of architect Marcel Breuer seated in the Whitney Museum of American Art, while more generally reflecting their firm Norman Kelley's interlinked interest in tradition and variation. Intentionally referencing the act of drawing, which is paramount to their design process, the transformed image was created on the gallery wall by painstakingly retracing line art on overlaid graphic transfer paper. The resulting image forced a spatially disassociated, false view "outside" and into the gallery, foregrounding two of the firm's chair designs—an effect further amplified by a vinyl shadow projection. The *Low-Back Settee* and *Rod-Back Side Chair*—two of the firm's seven-part Wrong Chair collection, which subtly modifies American Windsor chair types—embodied the firm's interest in novelty grounded in precedent.

In Geoffrey von Oeyen's installation, seventy-three obliquely configured, CNC-milled, hand-cut boxes framed renderings, drawings, and models of seven projects, some soon to begin construction. Each box was angled differently to pick up and reflect natural light, which activated the surfaces to provide a rippling sense of movement. The shifting proportion of the spacing between the boxes, intended "to give the sense of a still frame in an animation sequence," enhanced the dynamic quality of the array. The entire composition, proportioned as a golden rectangle, intentionally distorted the viewing plane of the rectilinear white box gallery. Von Oeyen subtly warped the combined surfaces of field to create a concave surface, drawing the viewer's focus toward the center of the composition while shaping the intersection between solid and void.

Conceived by Andrew Holder and Claus Benjamin Freyinger as elements that could make up the contents of a "living room, inside out," The LADG's installation held a collection of recent work that revisits and subverts familiar domestic forms to create unexpected and unconventional objects. Oversized, undulating "lumps" constructed of a gray concrete skim coat covering irregularly configured, CNC-cut plywood ribs opened to reveal a brilliantly red-hued, "primitive, upholstered interior" of fabric-draped insulation foam. Coffee-table books featuring the firm's projects topped sinuously restyled "occasional tables" straddled between and nestled within the lumps. Adjacent to the books were groups of "tchotchkes" designed by the firm—chess pieces, 3-D piglet scans, and other objects—that "re-present significant episodes from the recent work in miniature."

Linear bands of drawings, photos, and models documented recent projects by Jenny Sabin Studio, a practice that investigates the intersections of architecture and science by drawing on references from "matrix biology, materials science, and mathematics through the filter of crafts-based media including textiles and ceramics." Networks and natural systems informed two projects on display: *PolyMorph* and the *Greenhouse and Cabinet of Future Fossils*. Similarly, Sabin's *myThread Pavilion* explored linkages between the human body and adaptive materials through computation and the binary natures of weaving and knitting space. Sabin documented process and product with images illustrating installations constructed through generative design techniques that reference "natural systems, not as mimicry but as transdisciplinary translation of flexibility, adaptation, growth, and complexity into realms of architectural manifestation."

Adam Fure's installation, *Rocks*, designed for the exhibition, examined the materiality of objects and their form, addressing questions of scale, texture, color, and volume as well as possibilities for creating new "natural" forms. The project expanded his firm's ongoing experiments, which transform conventional substances through heat, finish, and color to create organic-looking objects. Exploring the fusion of digitally produced models and natural materials, the "rocks" were 3-D printed starch models coated in concrete, featuring pronounced surface articulation created by glazes, paints, and resin coating to emulate natural rocks. Fure produced an

accompanying system of graphic representations to develop fake histories for the specimens: photorealistic renderings showing ambiguously scaled rocks "in context" and images mimicking studio photographs, as well as pseudoscientific drawings exploring surface, section, and volume. As a whole, the project was intended to explore the potential (and architectural implications) of invented "natural" forms.

Nine equally sized display boxes held a selection of Kutan Ayata and Michael Young's work. The three-tier grid was divided into two wall-mounted rows of images set above a third plane of horizontal boxes holding 3-D printed architecture models. Backlit drawings of their Busan Opera House competition entry and an abstract drawing study were aligned above a series of projects rendered in photorealistic images and realized as objects. The firm's architectural designs find form in their models for a villa in Sharjah, their Busan Opera House proposal, and their Aalto University Masterplan competition entry. For Young & Ayata, the division of drawings, objects, and models "structures the installation and also describes the working mediums of the studio." The overlay of different modes of representation and conceptualization evidences the variety of design studies that inform their designs, reflecting the firm's guiding philosophy that architecture is not medium-specific.

Whether reconsidering historical typologies or inventing new materials and design methods, the combined projects demonstrated the intense effort behind the iterative design variations required to conceive, view, and review form. The winners' installations did not simply background or frame their work but instead located projects in a dynamic matrix, successfully answering the call to convey how the concept of overlay uniquely structures each firm's design process.

Biographies

In 2008 **Kutan Ayata** and **Michael Young** cofounded **Young & Ayata** to "explore novel formal and organizational possibilities in architecture and urbanism." The Brooklyn-based partnership is committed to experimentation and views "the reality of contemporary building as a provocation to the progression of experiments in form, material, and technology." The firm's work consists of both commissions and experimental research, as it seeks to engage "with contemporary cultural issues that influence and are influenced by our environment." Recent projects include the competition scheme of an opera house in Busan, South Korea, and a conceptual master plan for the Aalto University Campus Center in Helsinki, Finland. Ayata received a BFA in architecture from the Massachusetts College of Art in Boston and an MArch from Princeton University, where he was a recipient of the Suzanne Kolarik Underwood Thesis Prize. He is an adjunct assistant professor at Pratt Institute's Graduate Architecture and Urban Design Programs and a lecturer at the University of Pennsylvania. Young received a BArch from Cal Poly San Luis Obispo and an MArch from Princeton University, where he was also a recipient of the Suzanne Kolarik Underwood Thesis Prize as well as the Howard Crosby Butler Traveling Fellowship in Architecture. He is an assistant professor at the Irwin S. Chanin School of Architecture at Cooper Union and visiting lecturer at the Princeton University School of Architecture.

Established in 2004, **The Los Angeles Design Group (LADG)** is led by principals **Claus Benjamin Freyinger** and **Andrew Holder**. The firm works at all scales and has completed projects in California, Colorado, Hawaii, Minnesota, New York, Oregon, and the United Kingdom. The founders see their work as contributing to a "longer history of ideas" and draw on this history to craft unexpected solutions to conventional problems. Recent projects include installations at the Taubman College Gallery at the University of Michigan and several commercial interior renovations in New York and Santa Monica. Freyinger received his BA in art history from Boston College and an MArch from the University of California, Los Angeles, in 2005. Holder received his BA in political science from Lewis and Clark College and his MArch from the University of California, Los Angeles, in 2005. He is an assistant professor at the University of Michigan, where he was the 2012–13 Oberdick Fellow.

Adam Fure and his Ann Arbor design practice, **SIFT Studio**, enliven, in his words, "old substances through new treatments; composing new aesthetic mixtures from the matter at [one's] fingertips." Through these experiments, SIFT Studio "promotes architecture's unique capacity to shape experience, which is neither essentialized nor thought to be static and singular." Recent work includes a multimedia installation in Stuttgart, Germany, that transforms space, sound, and light into variable dimensions, and a conceptual mirror house that was a finalist for BOFFO Building Fashion's Linda Farrow competition in 2013. Fure received a BS in architecture from Taubman College of Architecture and Urban Planning at the University of Michigan, where he is currently an assistant professor, and an MArch with distinction from the Department of Architecture and Urban Design at the University of California, Los Angeles, in 2006.

Thomas Kelley and **Carrie Norman** founded the Brooklyn- and Chicago-based design collaborative **Norman Kelley** in 2012. Through their work, Kelley and Norman seek to "vulgarize, satirize, and reposition (lofty) material to elevate the ordinary." Recent projects include the Wrong Chairs, in which they "purposefully disrupt the notion of correctness" with stylized abstractions of the iconic American Windsor Chair, and *Shape Shape Evolution*, an interior playhouse for the Early Learning Play Foundation in Chicago. Most notably, Norman Kelley's drawings for Ignacio G. Galán were exhibited at the 2014 Venice Architecture Biennale and have been published in *Log 31: New Ancients*. Kelley received a BS in architecture with honors from the University of Virginia and an MArch from Princeton University. He was the 2013–14 winner of the Rome Prize in Architecture and is a clinical assistant professor at the University of Illinois at Chicago and a visiting critic at Syracuse University. Norman also received a BS in architecture with honors from the University of Virginia and an MArch from Princeton University. She is presently a senior design associate with SHoP Architects.

Jenny E. Sabin is principal of **Jenny Sabin Studio**, an experimental architectural design studio based in Philadelphia. Her work is at the forefront of a new direction for twenty-first-century architectural practice—one that investigates the intersections of architecture and science, and applies insights and theories from biology and mathematics to the design of material structures. She is assistant professor in the area of design and emerging technologies in the Department of Architecture at Cornell University, and director of the Sabin Design Lab, a hybrid research and design unit specializing in computational design, data visualization, and digital fabrication at Cornell's College of Architecture, Art, and Planning. She also cofounded LabStudio, a research and design network, with Peter Lloyd Jones. Sabin holds degrees in ceramics and interdisciplinary visual art from the University of Washington, and an MArch from the University of Pennsylvania, where she was awarded the AIA Henry Adams Medal and the Arthur Spayd Brooke Gold Medal for distinguished work in architectural design. Her work has been published extensively in *Architectural Review*, *Azure*, *A+U*, *Mark* magazine, *306090*, *10+1*, *Metropolis*, *American Journal of Pathology*, *Science*, the *New York Times*, *WIRED* magazine, and various exhibition catalogs and reviews. She coauthored *Meander: Variegating Architecture* with Ferda Kolatan in 2010.

Geoffrey von Oeyen is founder and principal of the Los Angeles–based practice **Geoffrey von Oeyen Design**, which has several projects in development across California, Texas, Georgia, and Puerto Rico. His work, as he describes it, "mediate[s] between the existing and the new with the aim of reframing and redirecting existing views, patterns, and orientations"; he characterizes this relationship within each project as "a dialogue that seeks to reveal essential geometric paradigms." Von Oeyen received a BA with honors in urban studies and minors in art history and history from Stanford University. He was a US/UK Fulbright Scholar at the University of Cambridge, where he obtained an MPhil in the history and philosophy of architecture, and received an MArch from the Harvard Graduate School of Design, where he accepted the Faculty Design Award and the Faculty Chair's Letter of Commendation. Von Oeyen teaches undergraduate- and graduate-level courses and serves as a studio faculty coordinator at the University of Southern California School of Architecture. In winter 2014–15, through a MacDowell Colony Fellowship, he developed research for Performative Composites: Sailing Architecture, an event he organized, curated, and moderated at USC to explore concepts and techniques in high-performance sailboat design and construction that could be used to solve formal, spatial, and programmatic problems in architecture.

Young & Ayata
Kutan Ayata and Michael Young

Realism is not the same as reality: it is an aesthetic argument about the relationship between reality and its representation. It might be assumed that this relationship could be natural, transparent; that the real could be accessed through images that resemble it effortlessly. But this is not the case—reality withdraws from the qualities presented through representations. A more accurate description of realism would be that it builds its aesthetic out of the tensions between reality and representation, between an object and its qualities.

Architecture includes, but is also more than, building. It involves multiple layers of mediations and representations that develop its realism. The drawing, the model, the photograph, and the text are all necessary in the development of an architectural project; however, no single medium defines the discipline of architecture. Rather than being medium-specific, architecture tends toward medium promiscuity. It requires multiple species of representation to build its aesthetic argument.

The practice of Young & Ayata operates on architectural conditions by drawing on the tensions that exist between multiple mediums. Digital models are built from three-dimensional curves that are more like drawings in space than material models. Line drawings are created from layered, colored vectors that build up a density of effects more closely associated with painting than drawing. Objects are fabricated in one material, but articulated through the qualities of another. Renderings of objects are inserted into photographs of paintings, altering the realism of the painting by becoming an integral part of it. Buildings reveal the strangeness of their sites by challenging the conventions through which those sites are represented. Textual arguments sit next to visual arguments and find alignments and frictions in their respective ideas.

The projects contained here are a sample of work at different scales developed by Young & Ayata over the past five years. The overall project that collects this work is an aesthetic argument regarding realism and estrangement within the arts. It could not have been completed without the generous help of many hands, including Asli Ayata, Caroline Young, Bryan Young, Thomas Heltzel, Luis Felipe Paris, Jonathan Alexander, Chrysokona Mavrou, Laura Carter, Abigail Happy Smith, James Hamilton, Stephen Ullman, Jim Stoddart, Alejandro Stein, Emmanuel Osorno, Sina Ozbudun, Steven Kocher, Sonia Flamberg, Walid Sehwail, Izodoro Michan, Mark Hernandez, Cole Belmont, Rodrigo Guajardo, and Mark Parsons.

Busan Opera House
Busan, South Korea, 2011

Operatic performance seeks to compress a multitude of specific art mediums—poetic narrative, dramatic performance, music (both vocal and orchestral), costume, lighting, set design—into a single temporal experience. But going to the opera is much more than the performance itself; it involves all the preliminary anticipatory experiences of the opera house. The entries, lobbies, stairways, foyers, bars, and restaurants are an integral part of the operatic event. This is where the architecture of the opera house becomes a crucial piece in the larger social, cultural, and aesthetic performance. Cultural institutions such as theaters, performance halls, museums, and operas provide and provoke much more than a functional display of artwork. They are participatory pieces in the complexity of societal relations, both in the direct experiences of each patron and through the larger urban conditions that surround the building.

We have responded to this challenge by making three specific interventions into the opera-house organization: First, the hierarchically striated auditorium seating staggers and compresses to become more intimate, egalitarian, and experiential. Second, the promenade of foyer/circulation is elongated into a mediating space for the participatory act of anticipatory congregation. Third, the pragmatic cruciform of performance stage and side stages becomes permeable, editable, and adaptable by taking on exhibition programs as seasons and schedules permit.

1: Aerial view
2: Box level plan

3: Lobby level plan
4: Main floor seating plan

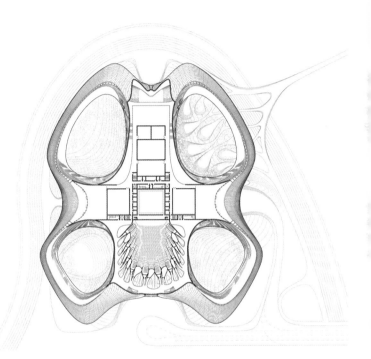

2

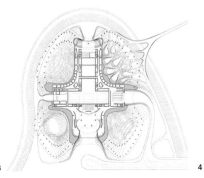

3

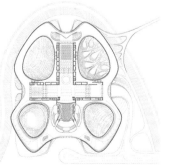

4

5: Opera box bridges

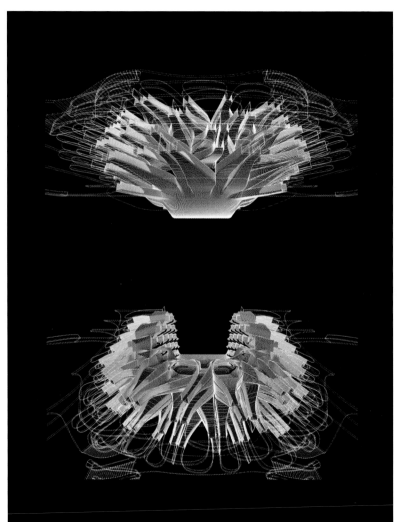

5

6: Front aerials

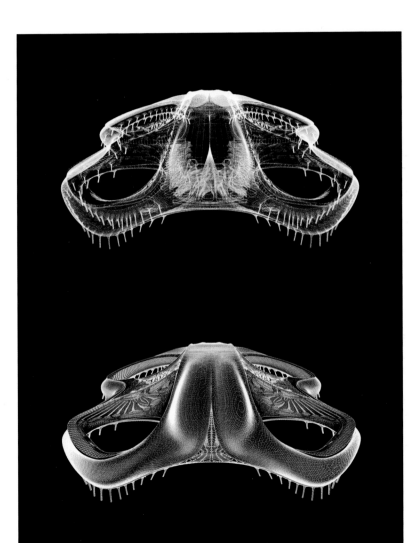

7: Bridge view
8–9: Promenade views

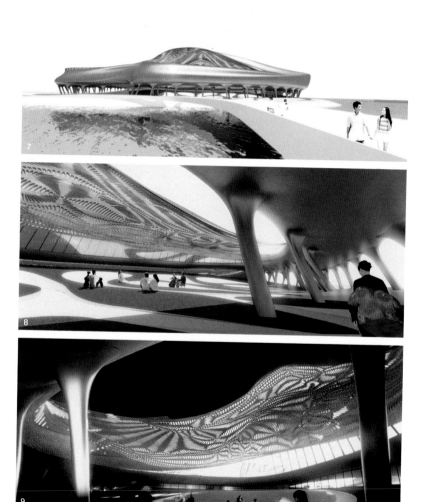

10: Model
11: Skin axonometrics

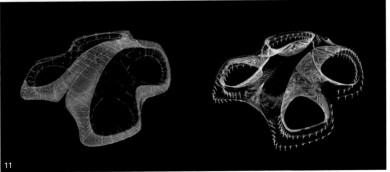

12–13: Lobby views to box bridges
14: Opera boxes

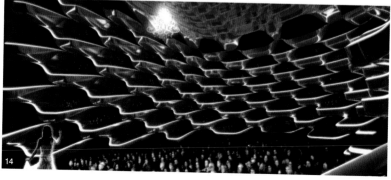

15: Box bridge model
16: Tiered boxes
17: Field of boxes

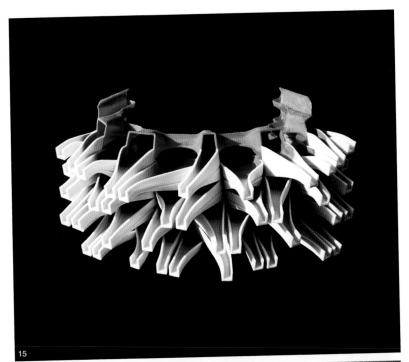

15

16

17

Villa at Al-Mezhar

Sharjah, United Arab Emirates, 2008

This project reimagines the courtyard typology for the arid climate of the Arabian Desert on a site located in a typically walled-in residential neighborhood of the city. The villa initially presents itself to the street as a levitating single volume perched on a solid stone plinth. The plinth holds the house's service and living spaces, which are organized around a central two-story courtyard. Within the courtyard lies a twenty-five-meter swimming pool that extends out into the backyard.

The upper volume consists of two generic boxes comprising sleeping quarters at each end. The solid boxes "soften" in the middle and dissolve into a double-layered trellis made of single-sized beams. The layers of the trellis are connected with five standard-length vertical steel rods to allow the structure to span the length of the shaded courtyard below. The varying distance of the layers creates moiré fields as light filters through the trellis. The quality and the nature of the moiré evolve through the day with the movement of the sun, producing different shaded zones in the courtyard.

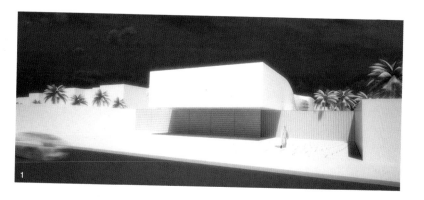

1

1: Upper courtyard view

2: Front view
3: Street view

4: Model

4

5: First-floor plan
6: Second-floor plan
7: Transverse section

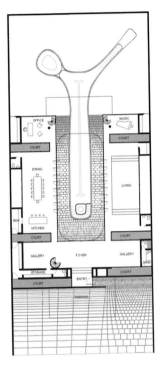

5

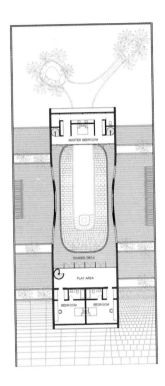

6

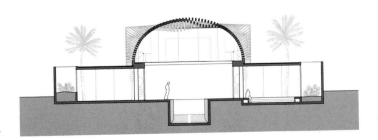

7

Aalto University Masterplan
Helsinki, Finland, 2012

The New Campus Center building and master plan for Alvar Aalto University is a dynamic hub of social, educational, and aesthetic exchange. Our design proposal originates from three concepts with respect to the planning of public space: the clearing of a public square, the filtering of circulation, and the establishment of a unique identity for the institution. In other words, the project desires to be simultaneously a void, a path, and an object. These three conditions are often at odds with each other, as they demand very different qualities from the architectural proposal.

    The public space develops from an initial gesture of two long bar buildings that house the School of Arts, Design and Architecture. These bars frame a plaza around an axis focused on the tower of Alvar Aalto's landmark auditorium. The initial symmetry of the plaza bends as it is inflected by the pressures of various circulation flows present in the site. The deflection is at its most extreme where it is closest to the Aalto building, suggesting that the existing building be understood as the object that disturbs the ideal symmetry of the campus center. The new design allows the context to become strange, needing to be understood in an alternate manner.

1: Site diagram: foliage
2: Site diagram: buildings and paths

3: Satellite view

4: Aerial view
5: Library axis view

6: Site plan

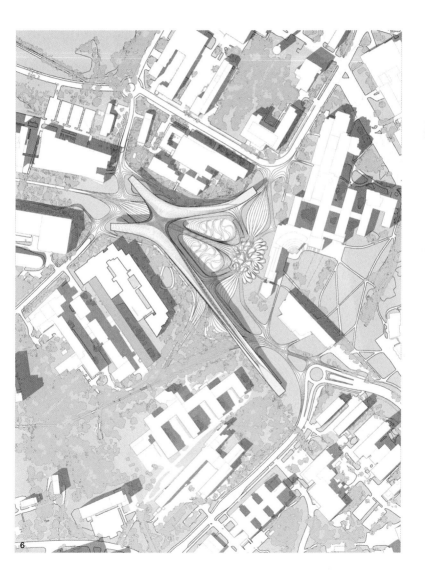

6

Drawings/Paintings
2009–2014

These drawings are an investigation of two long-standing representational themes: the tension between the sensory qualities of depth and the actual fact of flatness, and the difference between a line on a ground (drawing) and color variation in a matrix (painting).

The drawings are built from three sets of straight, two-dimensional lines. One set consists of tangent vectors along contours. The second set consists of normal vectors along the same contours. The third set consists of "furry" tangents that follow curves of constant tangency in relation to the first set of contours.

Once these lines are established, the work then proceeds on the variation of color, intensity, and saturation. These variables are judged in relation to the two questions above. When is there an increase in the tension between deep and flat? When does line become lost in tone? Each of these questions is related to issues of estrangement in realism. These representations are drawings in that they use line and only line, but they are manipulated and evaluated much more like paintings in that the lines accumulate as marks in a matrix developing movements of depth.

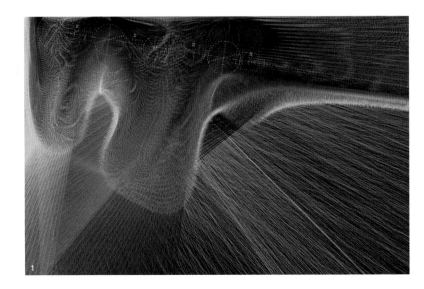

1: *Condenser*, 2012

2: *Guilded Splinter 73*, 2013
3: *Guilded Splinter 69*, 2013

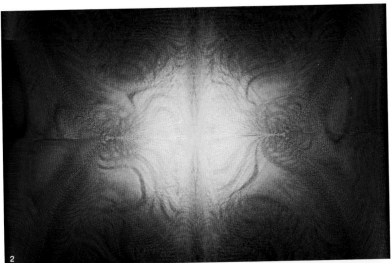

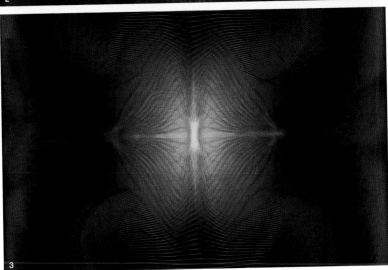

4: *Symmetry Series No. 7, 2012*

5: *Involutes: Silver Rocket*, 2010
6: *Involutes: The Sprawl*, 2010

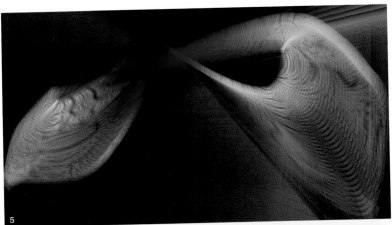

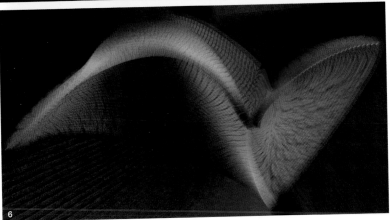

Still Life Interventions
After Pieter Claesz, 1641–2014

The project presented here is part of a larger series of experiments on objects and articulation that explore the production of a tension between an object's form and its surface qualities. The idea is that the two necessitate not a direct relation but a loose affiliation. These experiments are important testing grounds for the relations between ornament, decoration, material, and form. There are three phases to the defamiliarization: First, the figure is challenged through edge loss; second, the surface materiality and decoration are articulated to be in tension with the formal object; and third, the object is inserted into a scenario, changing the object as it also adjusts the reality in which it now exists. This last step explores the conditions of realism in a rendered image. For the project presented here, the new objects are inserted into seventeenth-century Dutch still-life paintings and allowed to take on qualities of these paintings. The goal is not to hide the objects behind something but to have them hide in plain sight. Their strangeness comes from being tensely accepted into their new contexts. The introduction of these objects begins to disturb those that already exist in the painting. The viewer begins to doubt the reality of everything in the image, intensifying the aesthetic qualities of realism.

1: Still life with lobster, silver jug, large Berkenmeyer   **2**: Fuzzy feather object
fruit bowl, violin, books, and sinew object, after
Pieter Claesz, 1641–2014

3: Breakfast with a crab and a fuzzy feather object,
after Willem Claesz Heda, 1648–2014

4: Sinew and geological objects

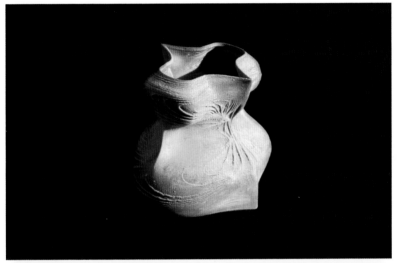

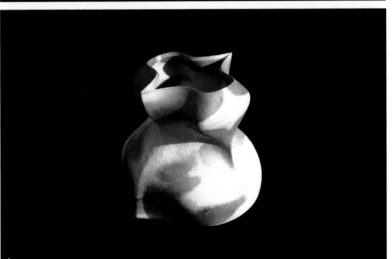

The Los Angeles Design Group (LADG)

Claus Benjamin Freyinger and Andrew Holder

Do not underestimate objects....Do not leave objects out of account. The world, after all, which is radically old, is made up mostly of objects.
—David Foster Wallace, *Infinite Jest*

Allow us a short story: In the beginning, The LADG was the corporate name for two people who agreed to follow a simple recipe: graduate, start a firm, build, and keep building until the record of our impact on the world was an accreted mountain of objects. And for the first seven years we were single-minded in this pursuit. We did nothing else: no competitions, no renderings, no paper architecture—only the production of concrete stuff. In our small office, we needed a way to build new things on top of an ever-expanding archaeology of our own making. Overlay allowed us to address the problem manually: this, on this, on this, on this, on...one thing placed on top of another.

Two propositions emerged from the accumulating pile. First, if the world is crowded with objects, architecture need not begin with the design of space or organization in the abstract. The crowd of physical things can fit together in very particular ways to produce space and organization as secondary, residual qualities. They appear in the slippages, misfits, and gaps between objects. In this scenario, familiar programs gain new resolve as they are squeezed between the physical artifacts that support them. New programs emerge with the urgency of happy survival strategies in a world of finite emptiness. Second, this world congested with objects is more interesting if it is flat. That is, in a flat world, objects can interact with one another more easily without categorical hierarchies that raise or lower status to the point of isolation. Our projects disregard category so that dissimilar things can strike up relationships by emphasizing the physical disposition of one thing against another. Objects herein are laid out like carpets across a floor, piled up like sandbags against columns, and plastered along walls like an encrustation of playbills. This flatness extends to the relationship between inanimate objects and living beings. Our ambition is to expand the register of architecture's communication with its audience to the point where inanimate material joins the audience as a member. We insist that objects gregariously invade space. We insist that objects deny distinction between the territory of the observer and that of the object. We insist that objects get in the way, reorganize rooms, please, infuriate, be useless, start conversations, remind people of other things, play tricks, demand bodily maneuvers, and offer utility in unexpected ways.

In the Garden Grows a Lump
Ann Arbor, Michigan, 2014

In the Garden Grows a Lump is an installation and exhibition of rare books on the picturesque. It proceeds from the observation that Sir Uvedale Price, author of the seminal *Essays on the Picturesque*, entertained a minor fascination with the word *lump*, but did not directly assert what they are. Lumps in the picturesque were used descriptively to modify other nouns like warts, pimples, and misshapen hills, but seldom, if ever, as objects in their own right. *In the Garden* attempts to build lumps.

The physical materials on display are straightforward and can be enumerated in a sequence from the ground up. There is the concrete floor of the gallery, seven occasional pillows, three lumps, four tables, and nineteen books. Physically, the books are resting on the lumps as a means of support, but conceptually, the lumps are not the site on which the books are placed—it's the other way around. The books suggest and intimate and imply a series of properties that lumps possess, but leave an indeterminate zone where direct evidence of lumps should be located. The built lumps in the gallery rest in this shadow of incomplete knowledge. Instead of citing history as a moral or formal justification for building, the show uses history as a site.

1

1: Section perspective

2: Plan perspective

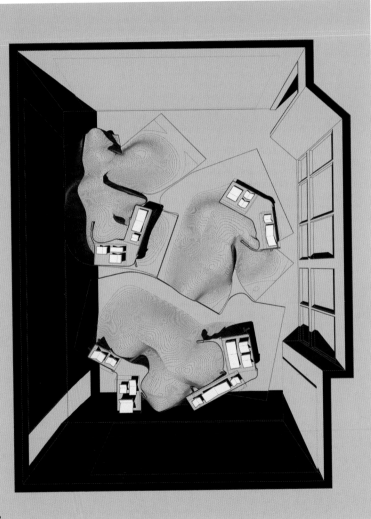

2

3: Reflected plan perspective

3

4: Exhibition panorama
5: Book display table

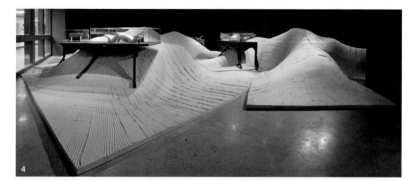

6: Detail underneath a lump (with pillow)
7: Detail of lump landscape (with pillow)
8: Detail of lump landscape
9: Detail of table interface with lump

10: Underneath a lump (with pillow)

48 Characters
Ann Arbor, Michigan, 2013

Consider, as a problem of material and form, a litter of piglets suckling at the teats of a plump sow. The language of formal analysis is not readily equipped to describe this situation. The disposition of one pig against another does not appear to be regulated by clear systems of repetition and adjacency. The pigs' bodies themselves resist decomposition as assemblages of skin and structure; they are too fat—all fat, in fact. What formal analysis struggles to rationalize, the languages of character and posture easily accommodate: the piglets nestle and suckle; the sow sprawls; obese bodies squeeze and abut one another. Using a method of plaster casting inside latex balloons, *48 Characters* offers a series of forms that aspire to the status of pig bodies by hugging, snuggling, and copulating their way toward the production of space.

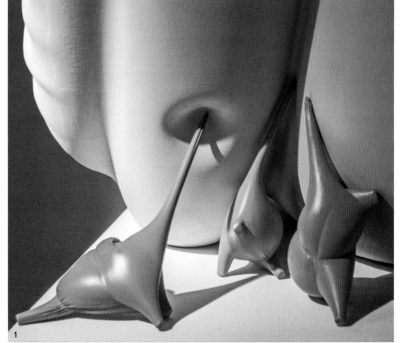

1

Photo courtesy of Eric Nelson

1: Detail of characters and pedestal   **2**: Two-way plan oblique

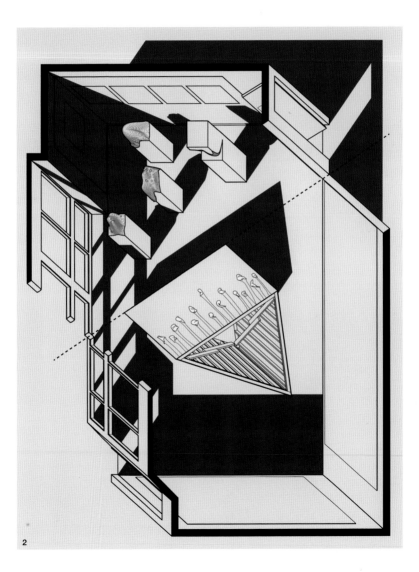

2

3: "Tummy" pedestal

Photos courtesy of Eric Nelson

4: Detail of hanging plaster balloon animal
5: Detail of "snuggle fit" between balloon animals
6: Detail of "snuggle fit" to pedestal
7: Installation view

8a–l: "Who's Under There?" formal analysis

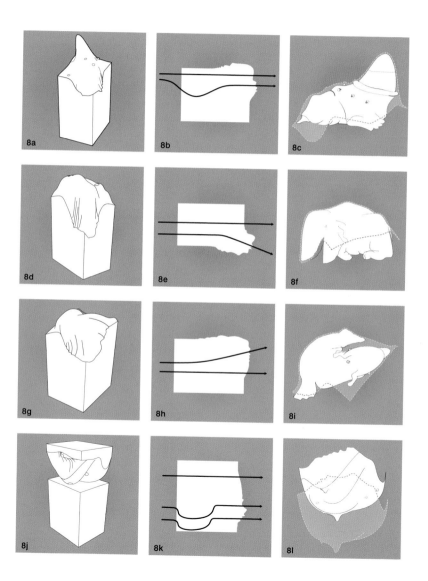

9: "Who's Under There?" character studies

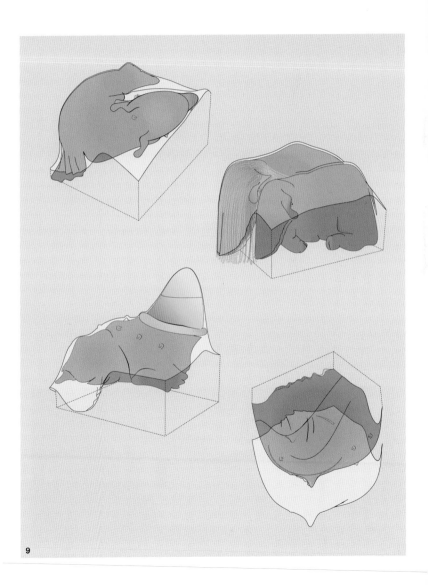

Surefoot Santa Monica
Los Angeles, California 2013

Surefoot is a retailer of custom-fit ski boots. Like most contemporary clients with more than one location, they require "brand coherence," or a certain kind of resemblance between stores irrespective of geography. This becomes a problem of how to repeat aesthetic and spatial strategies across wildly varying spaces and contexts. Our solution is an overlay of thin facades on the found condition of the "white box" retail interior. "Brand coherence" (in quotes because we are skeptical of the existence of "brands" apart from the literal, material instantiate) is articulated not only by the material we build but also by how we express its separateness from what came before. In a sense, we choose to reveal the falseness, the inauthenticity of our intervention as a way of building a kind of matter-of-fact trust with the occupants. While elements of the design may change from store to store, the aesthetics of thinness and deliberate overlay on a found condition are the guarantors of coherence across locations.

There are three components to the Santa Monica store: A curved dropped ceiling hangs several feet below the structure of the building shell, as though a thick tent cloth has been draped loosely from above. The display shelving is built into a thick plywood wrapper that covers two-thirds of the perimeter walls and has an irregular fit against the ceiling to create crevices, gaps, and awkward fits. A seating bench and equipment for digitally scanning customers' feet rest on the floor.

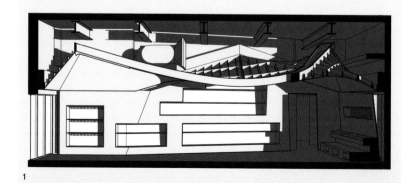

1

1: Section perspective

2: Two-way plan oblique

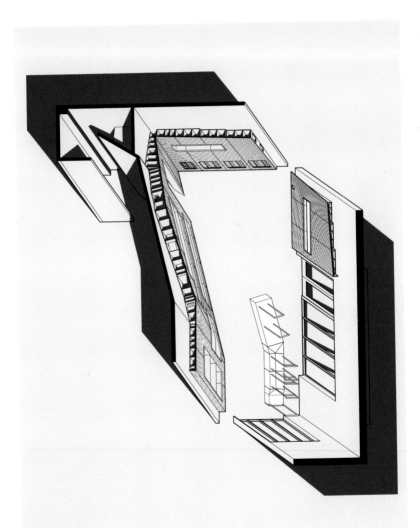

2

3: Store interior

3

4: Exploded perspective

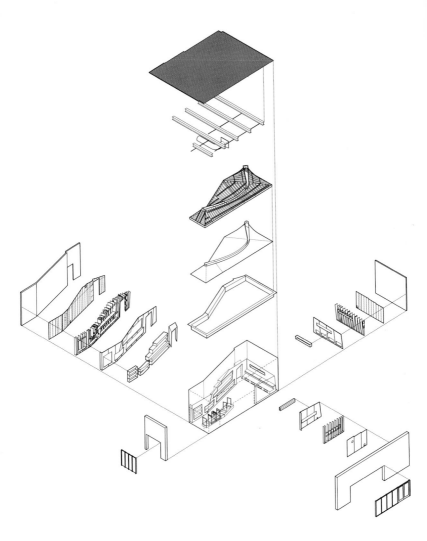

4

5: Detail of dropped ceiling

5

6: Detail of door through display wrapper
7: Display shelving
8: Gap between ceiling and display wrapper
9: Store interior

Accoutrements, Corpulence
Ann Arbor, Michigan, 2014

How does one know if a thing is fat or merely largish with a degree of rotundity? Making the distinction requires navigating an ever-finer system of differences: Is it round? How round? Is the roundness pert, upstanding, and symmetrical? Or does it have a down-rolling asymmetrical sag? Is the surface of this sag riffled with folds that indicate slippage between the skin and some underlying substance? And—beginning with an entirely different but equally necessary category of evaluation—after being poked, does it return to shape? How quickly does this shape return? Does a slight jiggle accompany the shape change?

Making the distinction between a fat thing and a merely largish, rotund thing also requires an understanding of profound consequences. To claim a thing is fat is to move it across a threshold between the animate and the inanimate. To claim a thing is fat is to ascribe life to inert matter.

How does one make a fat thing? If knowing the difference between fat and large requires an evidentiary system to test for fatness, do we then have to work backward through this same evidentiary system, meeting each of its endless conditions one by one in order to make a fat thing? No. There is another way. Corpulence has its accoutrements. It is contained in sweaters, diminutive jackets, casings that bulge and strain to satisfy minimum standards of decency. Fat things have their portraits painted. *Accoutrements, Corpulence* is a collection of these accoutrements and, by extension, fat things.

  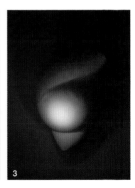

1: Chiaroscuro rendering
2: Chiaroscuro rendering
3: Chiaroscuro rendering

4: Plaster models in power-stretch nylon mesh

4

3 Books, 9 Tchotchkes, 3 Tables, 2 Lumps
New York, New York, 2014

This installation is a collection of recent work by The LADG. It is concerned with a problem that is faced by all emerging practices when they are asked to participate in a show: the firm is too new—too young to have produced anything that deserves to be treated as a survey or retrospective. One possible solution is to curate the work so that chronology and the self-importance of retrospective collapse, so that it is impossible to discern what is new and what is old, and the whole thing can be encountered afresh. In this case, we designed a few new objects and mixed them together with artifacts from old work to make a kind of living room, inside out. The emphasis is on the living room—old work has only the kind of incidental importance that is attached to the clutter of domestic space.

Like any living room, its contents can be enumerated by surveying objects from the top down. On top, three coffee-table books document projects that have been organized in clusters—*Installations and Speculative Work*, *Stores for Feet*, and *Built Work*. Adjacent to the books are a series of tchotchkes that re-present episodes from the recent work in miniature. The books and tchotchkes rest on a collection of occasional tables. These in turn rest on two lumps—a hilly landscape. Between the bottom surface of the lumps and the floor of the gallery is a primitive, upholstered interior.

An observer remarked that the project in the gallery does not look finished. We respond with a satisfied "thanks." The project declares in physical form the future ambitions of our practice: unfinished, open, and extensible, without being repetitive.

1

1: Section perspective

2: Plan perspective

2

3: Reflected plan perspective

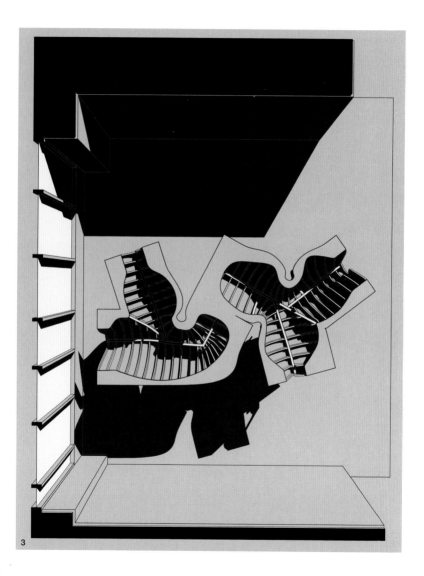

3

4: Detail of book on table
5: Detail of tchotchkes
6: Detail of table legs on lump
7: Installation view

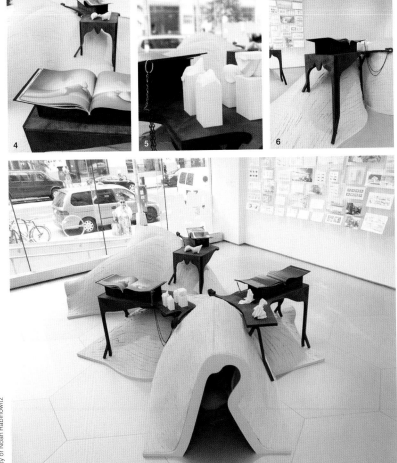

Photos courtesy of Noah Rabinowitz

SIFT Studio
Adam Fure

In my practice, overlay is operative in both the conception and reception of architecture. On the side of conception, my work overlays matter on form. Though these dimensions are ever present in architecture, their interconnection often follows disciplinary standards—materials filling in the geometric divisions of building or abstracted as constraints in fabrication processes. My material overlays are of another order; they are messy, rough, and textural. Whether in objects, installations, or buildings, these overlays pressure geometry to adapt to them, blurring clear profiles and relegating form to a supporting role. Thus, the paradigmatic separation of form and matter is muddied, smeared, and fused to produce objects seemingly born from both concerns. In my work, form is enmeshed in matter—copresent overlays of a single, synthetic artifact.

In terms of reception, my practice promotes architecture's unique capacity to shape experience, which is neither essentialized nor thought to be static and singular. Rather, human experience is understood as a complex, constantly shifting phenomenon: a two-way exchange between subjects and objects, each with their own autonomy and power to affect. This mutual enmeshment of subject and object is temporal and layered, made up of overlapping phenomena perceived in movement. These layers are exaggerated in my work: tactility overlays visuality, texture overlays color, image overlays illusion, and sound overlays space. This produces architecture where experiential expectations are constantly challenged, withdrawn, or altered, pulling architecture's audience inward, toward engagement. This pull is not the shock and alienation that comes from confronting the radically foreign, but the subtle allure of an expectation unmet, an aesthetic altered, or an illusion investigated.

Rocks
New York, New York, 2014

For the 2014 Architectural League Prize Exhibition, Overlay, I designed[1] new[2] rocks.[3]

[1]When a rock is designed, its properties are manipulable: texture can transform from surface to massing, holes can group to make faces, and coloration can be a mix of hues and iridescence. When a rock is designed, its properties are free to do new work.
[2]"New" rocks come with "new" natures. The old concept of nature is dead, offering three choices for a response: benignly neglect that fact, aestheticize ecological disaster, or offer alternatives. I choose the last, and these rocks are a beginning.
[3]These objects are rocks; not representations of rocks, not objects mimicking rocks— just rocks.

1: View of rocks in context

2a–c: View of rock groups
3: View of rocks in context

4: View of exhibition

5a–c: View of rocks in gallery
6: Drawings of rocks

6

Artifacts
Ann Arbor, Michigan, 2014

Initially, one might consider artifacts to be the consequence of some cultural process. Derived from the etymological roots of *arte* (by skill) and *factum* (to make), the term *artifact* indicates something made by humans that reflects the time, place, and traditions of its origin. As an architectural prompt, artifacts are a curious choice. When architects make things, those things typically represent something else—for example, models and drawings that depict a building. Artifacts, on the other hand, are what they are. Their mode of transmission—the way in which they convey things outside themselves—is not by representation but through embodiment, through strange auras that swirl around them echoing distant cultures. This is the ontology of the artifact.

But are there other ontologies? Can artifacts precede culture?

These objects follow those questions. As artifacts, they differ from traditional acts of speculative architecture, which enlist the full gamut of representation (models, drawings, and renderings) to produce totalizing images of alternative worlds. In contrast, the projective power of these artifacts stems solely from their physical traits: their idiosyncratic amalgamations of pockmarks, patinas, and profiles. This places great importance on aesthetics to affect culture, yielding a more modest political posture. These nine artifacts, born from material processes and bathed in iridescence, neither claim revolution nor confirm the status quo. Through a mix of conformity (cubic forms and colorful palettes) and exoticism (hazy figuration and arrested decay) they nudge culture, and its sensible dimension, from within.

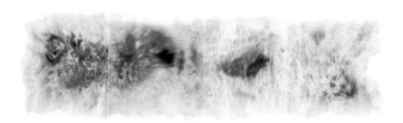

1

1: Unfolded elevation of Artifact 05   **2**: Artifacts 01–09

Mirror Mirror
New York, New York, 2013

Mirror Mirror, an entry for BOFFO Building Fashion's Linda Farrow competition and designed with Ellie Abrons of EADO, works likes a geode. Even after multiple sightings, geodes continue to amaze, as no one ever expects to find such colorful cores within ordinary rocks. Like the geode, *Mirror Mirror* conceals a bedazzling interior within a dark outer crust made from repurposed foam pieces stuck together and painted black. Inside is an angular array of taut, mirrored surfaces that infinitely reflect opalescent objects, which are meteor-like in appearance, but shinier, as if covered in glittering space dust. The objects' crusts are mostly coarse, but sporadically smooth where baroque-inspired masks appear to present Linda Farrow eyewear. The mirrors, some opaque and some translucent, line the interior walls and fold out to create cascading reflections, and a captivating ambiguity between what is real and what is illusion. One's experience is marked by simultaneous satisfaction and intensified desire—the pleasure of wearing luxurious eyewear and the tension that arises from objects withheld behind glass or present only as a reflected trace. In *Mirror Mirror*, what is commonly a singular, personal act of vision—seeing yourself in the mirror—becomes a collective performance of bodies and objects dancing around each other in a kaleidoscope of vivid imagery: a visual field of illusion and enticement.

1

1: View of interior (model)   2: View of interior (model)

3: Elevation
4: Section
5: Plan

3

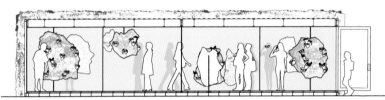

4

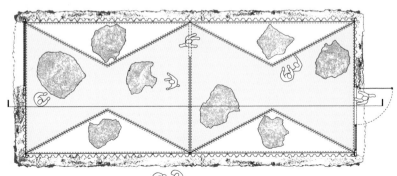

5

6: View of display rock texture
7: View of exterior (model)
8: Mock-up of display rocks

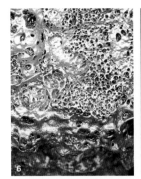

Hover
Ann Arbor, Michigan, 2012

Hover, a collaboration with composer Ashley Fure, is a study in perceptual thickness. Light, sound, and material are crafted not as separate layers of a multimedia project but as tangled strands of a multisensory knot. A base of stretched, burned, and painted cotton batting carves a series of compressed passageways. This same physical source is sonically sampled, spliced, and amplified through speakers embedded in the material walls. Across the space, colored gradations move from near white to deep metallic red. These changes are mapped to shifts in both the register (high and low) and the spectral density of the accompanying sonic reactions: blanched, pale walls are linked with soft white noise, while spaces saturated with color emit thick multiphonic screeches. Sensors tracking movement alter details in the sound, using presence and touch to thicken the acoustic air that hovers throughout.

In *Hover*, rhythm is articulated through the commingling and overlap of distinct temporalities. Separate sound files were designed for specific regions of the installation and are projected through localized speakers. The timbres and textures of each sonic arc respond to material shifts of texture, depth, and color while exhibiting distinct wavelike temporal structures, from amorphous washes of soft noise to more perceptually intrusive moments of gestural clarity. The sound files' temporalities both align and misalign with the natural rhythm of the participant's gait, piquing their awareness of the copresent mediums.

1: View of exit tunnel
2a–b: Detail view of batting

3: Detail view of batting covering branching
steel structure

3

4: Drawing illustrating relationship of batting to
branching steel structure

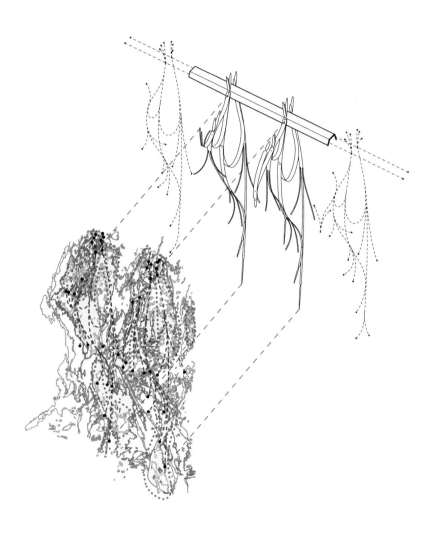

5: View of connection to ceiling
6: View of branching steel structure before application of batting
7: Detail view of branching steel structure supporting batting

8: Drawing illustrating geometry and flexibility of branching steel structure

5

6

7

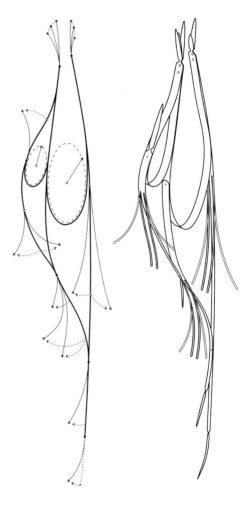

8

Stubble Step
Venice, Italy, 2012

This installation, designed in collaboration with Ellie Abrons of EADO for the Thirteenth International Architecture Exhibition in Venice, was a reimagining of a previous project situated in an abandoned house in Detroit. From the iconic Michigan Central Station to the vast fabric of abandoned single-family homes, the desolate state of Detroit's building stock is well known, having been extensively documented in the "ruin porn" that circulates through books, art blogs, and galleries. *Stubble Step* engages Detroit's blighted urbanity through materiality. Materials, like words, tell stories—in Detroit, these are somber tales: broken windows speak of abandonment; rotting wood, of neglect; burned walls, of indifference. Detroit's plight is written in the patina of its matter. Rather than fetishize or poeticize this blight, *Stubble Step* scripts new stories through novel approaches to old substances. Numerous experimental treatments were developed to estrange and alter common materials, producing an aesthetic that mixes natural decay with cosmetic embellishment. These saturated surfaces evoke timeless paradigms of entropy and educe unexpected associations, all the while eliciting tactile engagement from Stubble Step's many visitors.

 Stubble Step was one of five installations featured in *Grounds for Detroit*, a collaborative project designed by the group 13178 Moran Street for the Thirteenth International Architecture Exhibition, directed by David Chipperfield and titled Common Ground.

1: View of fabric detail

3: View of interior

2: View of wood detail

Veer

Stuttgart, Germany, 2012

Veer is a multimedia installation designed in collaboration with composer Ashley Fure that transforms space, sound, and light into variable dimensions of an experiential field. It is designed as five discrete zones, each characterized by a parsing, calibration, and alignment of their qualitative aspects—from material texture to sonic grain to spatial proportion. Physical characteristics in the material walls, made up of polyester batting wrapped around a branching steel structure, are mirrored in localized sonic responses that are triggered as participants move over pressure sensors embedded in the floor. Upon entry, visitors encounter an initial jolt of sensory stimuli. As they move through the installation, these sensations begin to coalesce into logical relations only to be undone as new temporal relations are revealed through different body movements. Bending and pushing through saturated matter, the participant initiates an aesthetic experience where subject and object emerge in a dynamic process of becoming. In this environment, no archetypal interactivity dominates; rather, the participant initiates a cascade of spatial/sonic relations structured with different temporalities. Thus the time of *Veer* is a manifold time, characterized by overlapping temporal arcs that fade in and out of focus in a dynamic play of experiential tension. Within *Veer*, space provokes movement, movement provokes sound, and engaged participants instigate an emergent perceptual form.

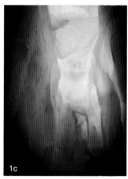

1a   1b   1c

1a–c: View of interior   **2**: View of entry

2

Michigan House
Hudson Hills, Michigan, 2012

Michigan House sits on a scenic riverbank in Hudson Hills, Michigan. The house's form, ground, and materiality express architecture's manifold relationship with nature. The north and south facades are thick, vegetal sheets draped from the house's frame like a fur coat. Inside, the facade is illuminated beyond glass walls and abstracted as vegetal patterns in shallow relief. The building's outer form is conceived as a dynamic line that "draws" its relation to the ground. Materialized in metallic trim, the line follows the building's outer edge, wrapping apertures and extending out into the landscape. The roof slopes from south to north and folds up at the corners, signaling entry and exaggerating the house's pitched shape. The exterior ground plane and interior floor heights further aid the experiential connection and separation from the site: the entry path descends through the vegetal facade to a sunken front door; the living room and kitchen hover above the surrounding site; and the master bedroom is partially submerged. On the whole, Michigan House draws on long-standing traditions of architecture expressing a connection to nature, yet no single approach dominates—rather, nature is framed in a multitude of ways, sequenced by the building's constituent formal and material variation.

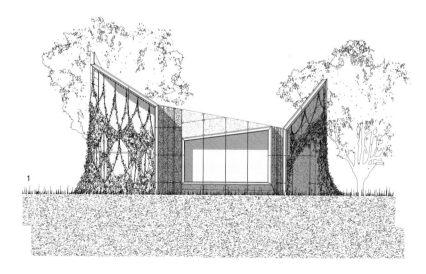

1

1: Elevation

2: Exterior view of entry

3a–b: Section

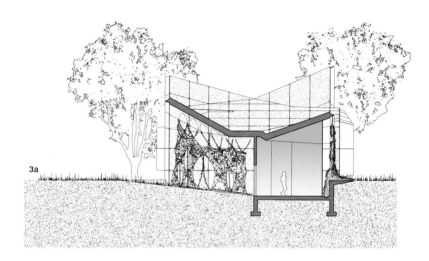

3a

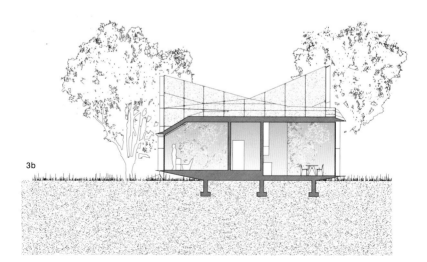

3b

4: Plan

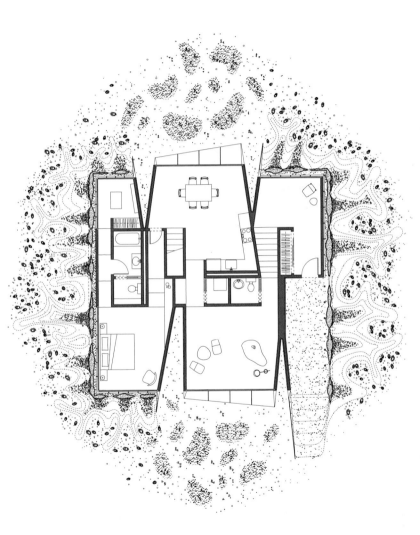

Norman Kelley

Carrie Norman and Thomas Kelley

Our architecture begins with a simple routine that unfolds in three acts. Act one begins with the presentation of something ordinary—an empty bowler hat, perhaps. Look closely and see that there is nothing distinct about this hat. It is black, oval, and hollow. Chaplin wore one. Trust is established. The second act, however, is meant to stir. Here, we take the seemingly ordinary object and transform it into something extraordinary— a white rabbit is pulled up from within the hat. The affect is unnerving for most, entertaining for some. It is at this precise moment of confusion, when the hat is at once a hat and not, that our audience is at its most attentive. Now for the third and final act. While this is the most prosaic of the three acts, it is the one that amazes most. We must return the hat to its point of origin before our audience shuffles away disoriented—the rabbit is placed back inside the hat, and with a twirl and a thwap of our wand, the hat returns to its original state. No more rabbit, just hat.

Applause. Bow. Replace audience. Repeat trick.

This is an all-too-familiar game in architecture known as a burlesque, whereby an ideality is constructed from which a shift is indexed to conjure a (fictional) narrative. Robert Venturi and Roy Lichtenstein played it. And so do we. We do not invent. Instead, we appropriate from within our ample discipline. Our overlays mettle (not meddle) with architecture's drawn histories—its canonical geometries, shapes, and stylized projections—to encourage layered and alternative readings. We favor the familiar and overlook the novel at all cost. We exercise precision by mining the consequences of error, and in doing so we refrain from overscripting our routine. This is where we advance our magician's model. Although the bowler hat returns to normal at the end of the show, it is never quite the same again. And like our hat, our audience exits having changed too. Like a good one-liner, our tricks aim to reassure expectation while imparting conspiracy. After all, you did see a rabbit just appear and vanish.

Chairs

A Collection of Wrong American Windsor Chairs (Built)
Buffalo, New York, 2013

The Wrong Chairs are an exercise in error. The collection consists of seven chairs that purposefully disrupt the notion of "correctness" by applying a medley of design mistakes to the iconic American Windsor chair. The Windsor chair, with its British roots, has become a symbol of colonial America—a chair that is unadorned and democratic in design. More importantly, however, it is also a forgettable chair. You might vaguely remember your grandmother having one in her kitchen. At first glance, the collection blends into the images we hold of domestic memories we've encountered at some point or another, but, at second glance, they're more unreasonable. In using an object readily recognized and embedded with nostalgia, the collection uses the Windsor chair as the control— a seemingly ordinary object—for the exploration of "wrongness."

Inspired by deceptive optics and adapting specifications from master craftsman Dr. John Kassay's drawings of eighteenth- and nineteenth-century American Windsor furniture, the collection plays an optical game (paused only when one is seated), taunting the observer to pay close attention and to interpret the visual boundaries of anamorphism, trompe l'oeil, and forced perspective. In provoking the observer to confront a traditional object transformed with intended error, the historical Windsor chair is resituated through a contemporary lens that is at once defective and functional.

Our aim is to discipline a potential for error toward new forms of making and observation. So please do sit down. The collection is at once both wrong and right. While the chairs may appear at times broken or unbalanced, they are structurally sound.

The collection was fabricated by Rives Rash in Burlington, Kentucky, and generously supported by Zoraida Tarifa-Pardo and the University at Buffalo School of Architecture and Planning.

1

1–2: Modified by authors from John Kassay,
*The Book of American Windsor Furniture: Styles
and Technologies* (Amherst: University of
Massachusetts Press, 1998).

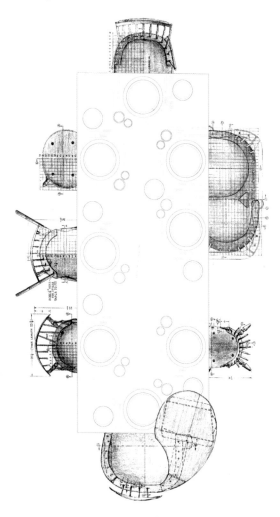

2

3: *Step-Down Armchair*, detail

4: *Comb-Back Writing-Arm Chair*
5: *Step-Down Armchair*
6: *Continuous-Bow High Chair*
7: *Two-Place Low-Back Settee*

8: *Rod-Back Side Chair*
9: *Comb-Back Side Chair*
10: *Tall Stool*

Playhouse

A Shape Shape Evolution for the Early Learning Foundation (Built)
Chicago, Illinois, 2014

While most playhouses are geared to producing a small-scale interior environment for children, the design of a playhouse for a bilingual preschool in Chicago's Old Town neighborhood turns the familiar diagram inside out. By wrapping an existing column with a graphic relief and eight soft play shapes, the new structure enlivens the school's existing playroom—a new interior within an existing one.

From within the playroom one observes that the exterior of the playhouse is patterned with an "educational relief" graphic. Playing on a preschooler's ability to recognize basic figuration, the pattern transitions vertically in scale and in depth so that the primitive geometries (triangles, squares, and circles) of the play shapes located at the bottom blend to produce more recognizable figures (animals, stars, and lucky charms) at the structure's top. Once the play shapes have been removed, the structure is accessible for children to stage puppet shows and teachers to store materials. Instead of curating a single and static play environment, the mobile and light play shapes produce smaller-scale playgrounds throughout the playroom.

Overall, the playhouse resolves its concise set of functional and educational requirements through a simple framework of visual and physical evolution through its approach to pattern, color, and tactility.

The playhouse was generously supported by Judge Dice and Emily DiCesaro.

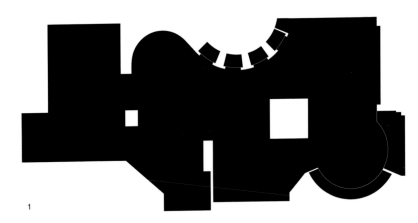

1

1: Site plan

2: Plan, closed
3: Plan, open

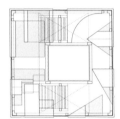

2

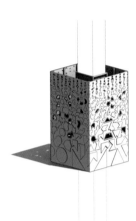

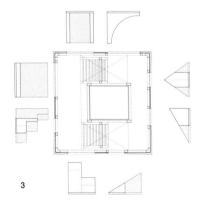

3

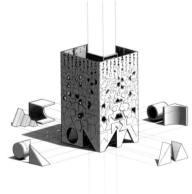

4: Exterior view of south elevation with play
shapes removed

5: Unrolled elevation of relief graphic
6: Play shapes are flipped and combined to
produce a variety of play scenarios

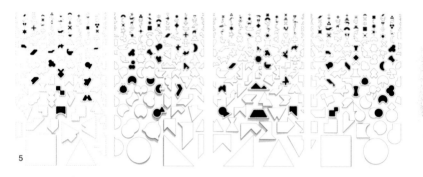

5

6

Barrel

An Optical Object for Edgar Rubin and the Herradura Tequila Company (Built)
Chicago, Illinois, 2013

If you squint hard enough, your focus will be drawn to the barrel's stout exterior
silhouette, an outline with two perfectly symmetrical contours that appear to bow
outward. All the object's signifying "barrel" features—six metal straps and twenty-two
vertical seams—have been masked or removed to underline this iconic outline. Now
allow your eyes to relax. Are you drawn to a new set of contours? The false silhouette
no longer gives the impression of a portly character expecting to be drained, but rather
a sinewy black figure—symmetrical now only from one angle. Look even closer, and
you may also see the projection in reverse. The original object, once controlled and
purely functional, is now bistable or, worse yet, ambiguous. It aims to invert its physical
proportions by pulling its waist inward—no longer a barrel, but a vase. But that's not
entirely true either. The visual game is one of multiple contradictions. What do you see?

The object's two-dimensional characters make reference to Danish psychologist
Edgar Rubin's iconic 1915 gestalt image of a vase and/or two mirrored faces in profile.

The barrel was fabricated by Ryan Palider and commissioned by the Herradura Tequila Company.

1

2

1: Edgar Rubin's reversible drawing

2: Norman Kelley's irreversible version of Rubin's drawing

3: 360-degree rotational sequence

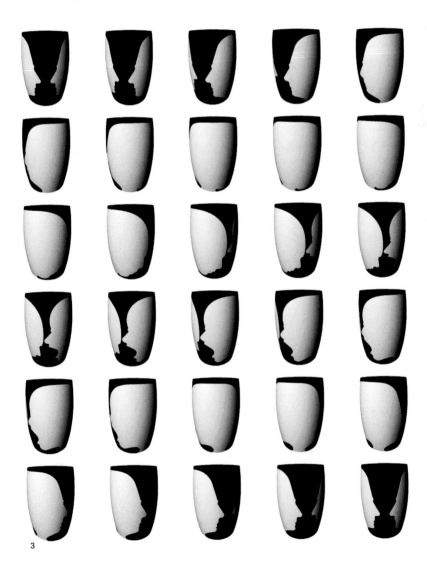

3

4a–i: Fabrication sequence

5: Symmetrically mapped image
6: Asymmetrically mapped image

Balloons
A Sustainable Art Installation for the Land Art Generator Initiative (Proposal)
Fresh Kills Landfill, New York, 2012

But Phileas Fogg, who was not traveling, but only describing a circumference...
—Jules Verne, *Around the World in Eighty Days*

It is a common misconception that Phileas Fogg's journey in *Around the World in Eighty Days* was by hot air balloon. The iconic image, however, fulfills a visual nostalgia for the whimsical beauty of a floating mass. Despite the misreading of Verne's text, the image is far too satisfying to pass up, and we accept the error. The aim of this project is to couple the image of an oversized helium-filled teardrop with a nuanced application of wind energy technology. While the balloon's image and subsequent geometry are the primitives to this proposal, the deployment on the Fresh Kills site ignites an interest in the oversized and the attenuated. Thousands of airborne wind turbines are embedded in conic hair follicles, which are applied normal to the balloon's curved surface. Skewing the iconic image of Verne's buoyant transportation, the aim of *N.A.W.T. (Normal Axis Wind Turbine) Balloons* is not flight or expedition. But through its multiplication and reconfiguration, it may be able to produce new, yet familiar, collections of iconicity. It is our belief that it's not important that the method of travel in Fogg's journey is often depicted falsely but that it continues to strike a chord with the eyes, both young and old.

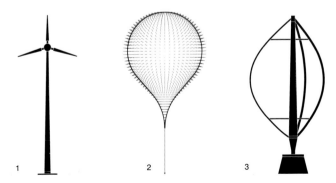

1   2   3

1: Vertical axis wind turbine
2: Normal axis wind turbine
3: Horizontal axis wind turbine

4: Elevation view of child running through field holding cluster of *N.A.W.T. Balloons*

4

5: Cutaway elevation of *N.A.W.T. Balloons* prototype
(patent pending)

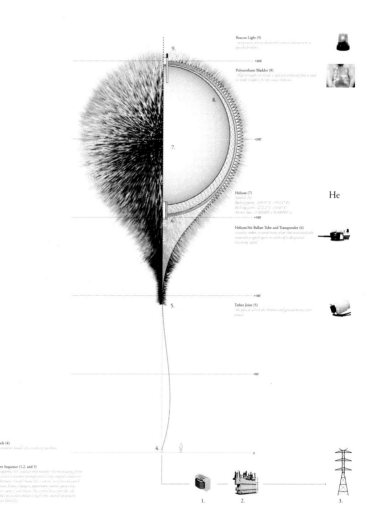

Beacon Light (9)

Polyurethane Bladder (8)

Helium (7)

He

Helium/Air Ballast Tube and Transponder (6)

Tether Joint (5)

Winch (4)

Power Sequence (1, 2, and 3)

6: Treasure map, axonometric view of balloon
assemblages across site

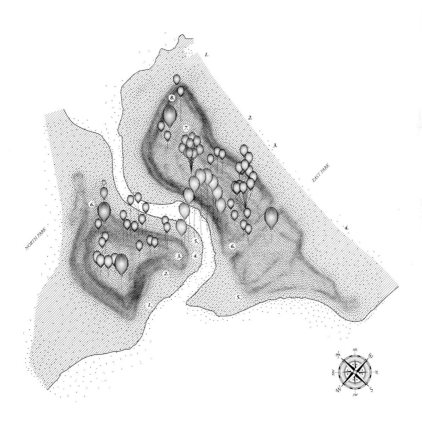

Freshkills Park

NORTH PARK
1. *Exhibition Area for Temporary Displays*
2. *Eco-Education Exhibit and Display Garden*
3. *Methane Movies and Media Screens at the Flare Stations*
4. *Exhibition Area for Temporary Displays*
5. *Energy Transformer*
6. *Rock Basin Garden*

EAST PARK
1-4. *Berm Overlook*
5. *Sunken Forest*
6. *Flare Station Projection Screen*
7. *Morphing Timelines*
8. *Sites for Celebration*

Folly

A Game of Musical Chairs (Proposal)
Socrates Sculpture Park, New York, 2012

We believe that when it comes down to hashing out a disagreement, receiving congratulation, or bearing some difficult news, most people opt for the face-to-face sit-down. The rationale is simple: intimacy. Whether it's good news (a promotion!), bad news (you're fired!), or no news at all (a lover's gaze, perhaps?), it will always be more intimate when the registration of affect is experienced firsthand. The pairing of both the visual and the approximate is the ultimate human tell-all. Common sense indicates that much of our social anxiety stems from our ability (and inability) to receive and present information through our visages, yet this is mildly incorrect. For it is the folly of the face, or rather, the notion that a face-to-face exchange is limited to the purely visual, or purely adjacent. A face-to-face exchange must account for a variety of controls that include but are not limited to psychological contingencies, posture, sensory conditions such as aural (not oral) stimulation, and physical proximity that mesh to form a (more) complete definition of what constitutes a "social interaction."

Here we have focused our attention on a singular misreading of the face-to-face exchange: the axis. By definition, the positioning of bodies within a face-to-face exchange is somewhat self-explanatory: two players face opposite each other. Such a simple idea has been made popular by performance artist Marina Abramović and layered-transparency guru Dan Graham. For both artists, the goal is to provide a visual commentary on social interaction and its cultural perception while maintaining a singular reading of the axis. For example, in Abramović's installation *The Artist Is Present*, the artist faced off against museum visitors (often strangers) in silence. In our proposal, however, the axis is made more flexible by compositing groups of axes to include not only the linear but also the parallel, the oblique, the perpendicular, the opaque, and the through axis. Once its definition is no longer restricted to unobstructed lines of sight, the axis may curate an audience as opposed to simply orient a pair.

1

1: Site-plan assemblages

2: Face-to-face components

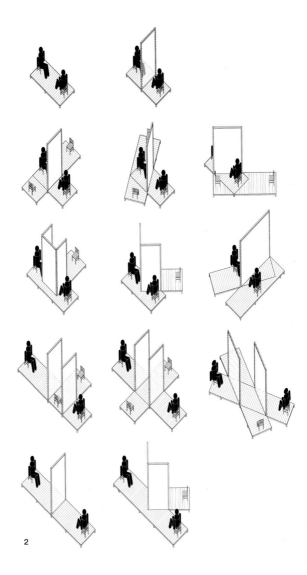

2

3: Axonometric view of musical vs with music on

3

4: Axonometric view of musical chairs with music off

View

An Anamorphic Projection of the Arthur and Janet C. Ross Library (Built)
Rome, Italy, 2014

On the second floor of the American Academy in Rome's 1914-designed McKim,
Mead & White Building exists a peculiar hallway. The hallway measures approximately
one hundred feet long, twelve feet high, and, believe it or not, thirty-two inches wide.
On the eastern side of the hallway one finds a row of eight identical doors that
open onto offices of an elite group of scholars. Looking west down the hallway, one
finds nothing at all, save a blank wall, that runs the full length of the cramped space.
If one were able to look through this blank wall, one would be looking into the main hall
of the two-story Arthur and Janet C. Ross Library. The hallway and the library are
separated by a wall but conjoined in plan and section.

   Using graphite transfer paper and some ink highlights, the hallway is reconditioned
and expanded. When standing at the northern end of the hallway looking south, one
is afforded a view looking down into the library only one level below. The two spaces
are collapsed into each other through a single projection, or view, using the often-
derided technique of anamorphosis, or a style of drawing that allows for an image or
object to be reconstructed only when observed from a specific vantage point. The
wall is no longer a wall, but now a false window peering into a real, yet false, space.

The drawing was generously supported by the American Academy in Rome.

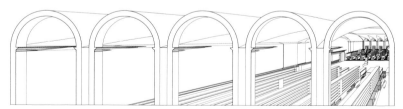

1

1: View of library in elevation

2: View of library in one-point perspective

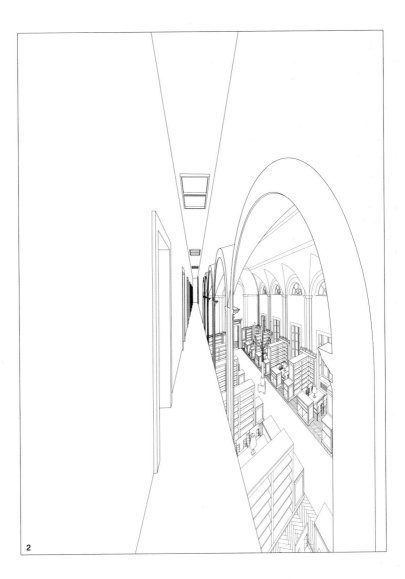

2

3a–b: Photographs of wall detail

4: Photograph from optimal vantage point

4

Jenny Sabin Studio
Jenny E. Sabin

Jenny Sabin Studio is an experimental architecture and design studio based in Philadelphia, with strong links to the Sabin Design Lab at the Cornell University Department of Architecture. The studio investigates the intersections of architecture and science, and applies insights and theories from biology and mathematics to the design, fabrication, and production of material structures. Jenny E. Sabin's practice and research are invested in developing an alternative material practice in architecture through the generative fabrication of the nonlinearities of material and form across disciplines. Biology presents useful conceptual models to consider, where form is in constant adaptation with environmental events. Here, geometry and matter operate as an active elastic ground—a datascape—that steers and specifies form, function, and structure in context. Seminal references for Sabin's work include matrix biology, materials science, and mathematics through the filter of crafts-based media including textiles and ceramics. Her work, carried out in collaboration with multiple colleagues , from science and engineering, attempts an analogous deep organicity of interrelated parts, material components, and building ecology. In discerning which effects and materials are actually scalable, her practice and research operate across three phases. The first includes new tools and novel methodologies for modeling complex behavior; the second entails architectural prototyping at the human scale; and the third operates at the scale of ecological building design. This three-pronged approach engages materiality and geometry in multiple contexts, as active overlays composed of dynamic data. Networks inform three featured projects: *Branching Morphogenesis*, *eSkin*, and *PolyMorph*. As does the *myThread Pavilion*, her research diversifies into linkages between computation and the binary natures of weaving and knitting, which influenced parallel innovations such as the contemporary computer and digital space. By investigating loops that filter data sets through material organizations, Sabin's work seeks to form a bridge between the human body and technology as an active overlay that influences and contributes to an alternative material practice in architecture.

    The following pages showcase Sabin's work and research over the past six years in the context of her studio practice and transdisciplinary collaborations. Generative design techniques emerge with references to natural systems, not as mimicry but as transdisciplinary translation of flexibility, adaptation, growth, and complexity into realms of architectural manifestation.

Branching Morphogenesis

SIGGRAPH, Los Angeles, California, 2008
Ars Electronica, Linz, Austria, 2009–2010

Branching Morphogenesis explores fundamental processes in living systems and their potential application in architecture. The project investigates part-to-whole relationships revealed during the generation of branched structures formed in real time by interacting lung endothelial cells placed within a three-dimensional matrix environment. The installation materializes five slices in time, capturing the force network exerted on the matrix by the networking vascular cells. The time lapses manifest as five vertical, interconnected layers made from over 75,000 cable zip ties. Gallery visitors are invited to walk around and in between the layers, thus immersing themselves within a newly created datascape, fusing dynamic cellular change with human occupation, all through the constraints of a ready-made. The final artifact is a synthesis—a biosynthesis—for people to inhabit and experience.

The aim of this project is to sequentially model the networking process in vitro and in silico, and then to abstract this process into experimental architecture. To approach this, we have studied the parameters that govern branching morphology in response to the underlying extracellular matrix (ECM), and how this alters cell-cell and cell-ECM interactions during networking. We have explored potential parameters that prohibit networking behavior, including intercellular communication, environmental instigators, and cellular geometry. Through the investigation of controlled and uncontrolled cell tissue biological models, parallel models work to unfold the parametric logic of these biological and responsive systems revealing their deep interior logic. The result is a component-based surface architecture that abstracts and embeds both environments (context) with deeper interior programmed systems.

In collaboration with Sabin+Jones LabStudio, University of Pennsylvania; and Jenny E. Sabin, Andrew Lucia, and Peter Lloyd Jones.

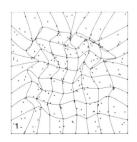
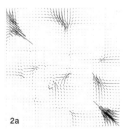
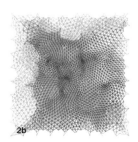

1: Simulation of parameters that govern branching morphology in response to the underlying extracellular matrix

2a–b: Human scale construction templates for the installation

3a–g: Design process–highlighting abstraction of cellular data through digital simulation and the final material system at human scale

3a

3b

3c

3d

3e

3f

3g

4a–d: Details of the final installation. The bottom left image won the AAAS/NSF International Visualization Challenge and was featured on the February 19, 2010, cover of *Science* magazine.

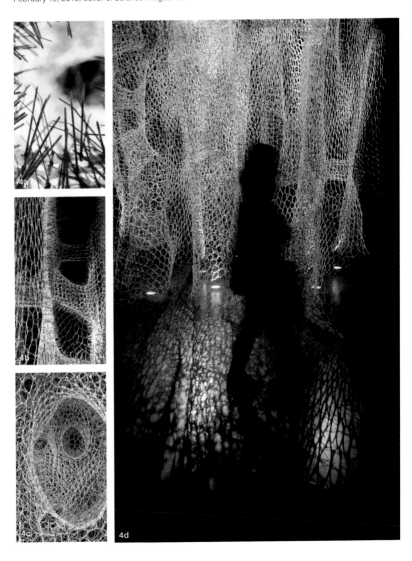

5: The densest areas of the network are connected
with tubes composed of cable ties, connecting one
surface to the next.

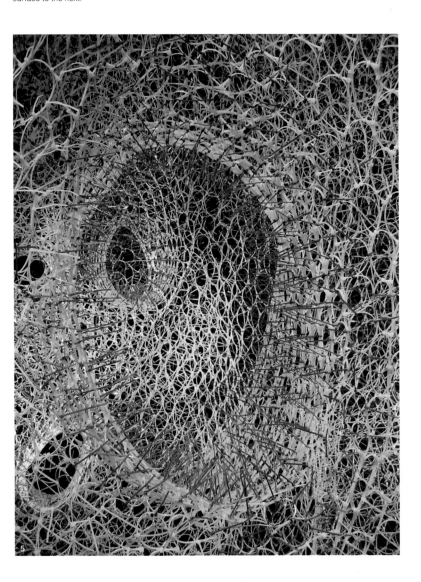

eSkin

Core Research
University of Pennsylvania and Cornell University, 2010–2014

We ask: How might architecture respond to issues of ecology and sustainability whereby buildings behave more like organisms in their built environments? In turn, what role do humans play in response to these changing conditions? The *eSkin* project starts with these fundamental questions and modes of design thinking, and applies them toward the design and engineering of programmable and adaptive materials to be integrated with existing and new building facade assemblies.

The goal of the *eSkin* project is to explore materiality from nano- to macroscales based on the understanding of nonlinear, dynamic human cell behaviors on geometrically defined substrates. Through the *eSkin* project, insights as to how cells can modify their immediate ECM microenvironment with minimal energy and maximal effect are being investigated and applied to the biomimetic design and engineering of highly aesthetic, passive materials, as well as to sensors and imagers that will be integrated into responsive building skins at the architectural scale.

This project represents a unique avant-garde model for sustainable and ecological design via the fusion of the architectural design studio with laboratory-based scientific research. In turn, this project benefits a diverse range of sciences and technologies, including the construction of energy-efficient and aesthetic building skins and materials. The synergistic, bottom-up approach across diverse disciplines, including cell-matrix biology, materials science and engineering, electrical and systems engineering, and architecture, brings about a new paradigm to construct intelligent and sustainable building skins that engage users at an aesthetic level with minimal energy consumption.

In collaboration with Sabin Design Lab, Cornell University; Andrew Lucia, Architecture, Cornell; Shu Yang, Materials Science and Engineering, University of Pennsylvania; Jan Van der Spiegel and Nader Engheta, Electrical and Systems Engineering, University of Pennsylvania; and Kaori Ihida-Stansbury and Peter Lloyd Jones, Pathology and Laboratory Medicine, University of Pennsylvania. This project is funded by the National Science Foundation under the Emerging Frontiers in Research and Innovation (EFRI) Science in Energy and Environmental Design (SEED) umbrella.

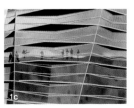

1a–c: *eSkin* prototypes and visualizations: board display and components of human-scale interactive prototype; simulation of *eSkin* optical properties; building-scale speculation of *eSkin* features

2a–j: Nonlinear nano- to micro-scaled material properties and effects of *eSkin* generated by human cells on defined geometric surfaces. Visualizations of key material features and functions revealed by cells for sensing and control at the building scale.

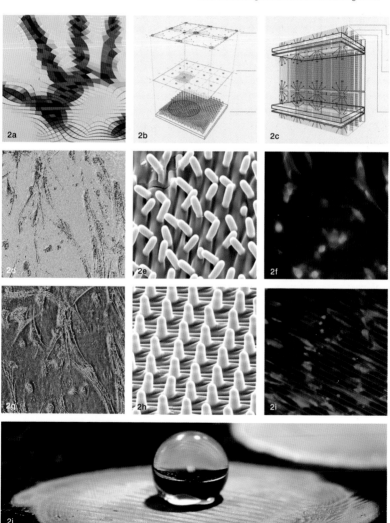

3a–e: *eSkin* human-scale interactive prototypes
and architectural speculations featuring color and
transparency change, sensing-based color change
because of user input and a tunable window

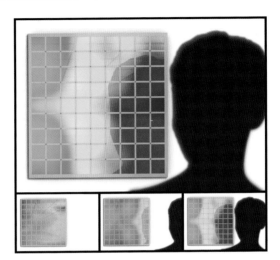

3a

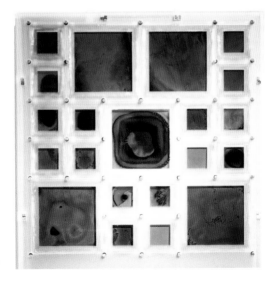

3b

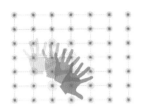  

3c

3d

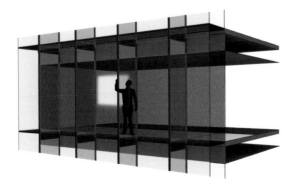

3e

4: Simulation of interior building partition of *eSkin*
optical properties

4

Greenhouse and Cabinet of Future Fossils

Greenhouse Pavilion, Jefferson Garden, American Philosophical Society Museum
Philadelphia, Pennsylvania, 2011

Through its material configuration composed of multiple woven surface assemblies—
some natural and others synthetic—the *Greenhouse and Cabinet of Future Fossils*
attempts to gather, digest, and disseminate information about nature while
incorporating digital fabrication and algorithmic design techniques to produce a
greenhouse of the digital age. The pavilion structure is populated with cold-frame
modules and futuristic ceramic and 3-D printed curiosities, prefabricated and
assembled in the Jefferson Garden, Philadelphia. Taking inspiration from the artifacts
in the exhibition Of Elephants and Roses: Encounters with French Natural History,
1790–1830, the *Greenhouse* encapsulates the open and dramatic spatial attributes of
the outer-body in the field—defined as a three-dimensional tapestry of organic and
synthetic material layers—while expressing the closed and steady gaze of the
inner-body confined within the boundaries of the cabinet, geometrically materialized
as a wall grid of cold frames and display vitrines.

The entire structure was prefabricated locally in Philadelphia and assembled
on-site. The primary rib system consists of CNC-cut, recyclable high-density
polyethylene plastic parts, and 100 percent recycled plastic lumber board sections
serve as a cross-bracing system. The structure is populated with live vines, and
each cold frame houses a variety of plants and soil. The interior gallery within
the structure houses the *Cabinet of Future Fossils*, a modular system holding newly
fabricated 3-D printed and ceramic artifacts inspired by nature, complexity, and
generative design processes.

The *Greenhouse and Cabinet of Future Fossils* was commissioned by the American
Philosophical Society Museum and funded by Heritage Philadelphia Program, a
program of the Pew Center for Arts and Heritage.

Architectural Designer: Jenny E. Sabin; Consulting Engineer: Tristan Simmonds; Fabricator: Mikael Avery,
Draft Works LLC; Design and Production Team: Mikael Avery, James Fleet Hower, Jason Jackson,
Anooshey Rahim, Kathryn Rufe, and Meagan Whetstone

1: Generative design strategy based on knot topologies

2a–b: Diagram of material systems and final drawings of the greenhouse

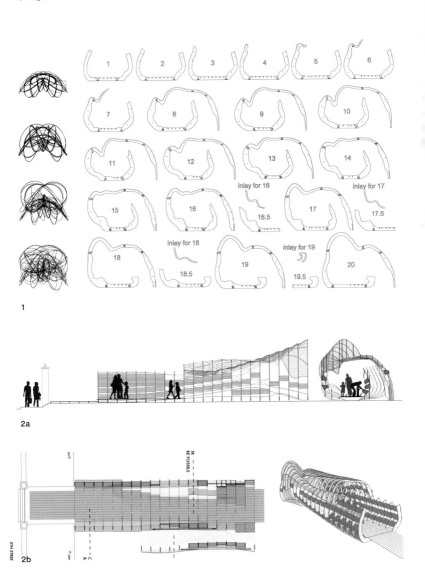

3a–i: Digital models and details of the installed and planted greenhouse

4a–b: Interior view and overall shot of the
Greenhouse and Cabinet of Future Fossils

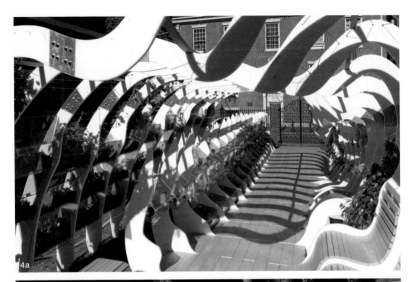

PolyMorph

Permanent collection, Frac Centre, Orléans, France
Originally on view as part of the Ninth Archilab, Naturalizing Architecture, 2013

This project showcases next steps in the integration of complex phenomena toward the design, production, and digital fabrication of ceramic form in the design arts and architecture. It interrogates the physical interface between networking behavior and fabricated material assemblies in order to address novel applications of nonstandard ceramic components toward the production of 3-D textured prototypes, screen systems, and spatial structures.

Key to this design research is the exploration of new tectonic organizations for application at the architectural scale. Importantly, the plastic nature of clay offers up a potent material solution to contemporary generative design processes in architecture, which frequently feature organic and natural forms of increasingly complex expression and ornamentation. Essential part-to-whole relationships abstracted from mathematical and natural systems are explored through the design and 3-D printing of one-to-one-scale nonstandard components. A bespoke script based on networking behavior and recursive properties generates *PolyMorph*. The density of the network is constrained by material properties inherent to working with clay. The nodes within the network are spatialized through three distinct but connected components that are held in continuous compression through an internal steel tension network to form a large, rigid spatial structure. Together, the components feature over 250 different connection combinations.

This project was funded jointly by Jenny Sabin Studio, the Pew Fellowships in the Arts, and the PCCW Affinito-Stewart Grant at Cornell University.

Architectural Designer: Jenny E. Sabin; Design and Production Team: Martin Miller, Jillian Blackwell, Jin Tack Lim, Liangjie Wu, and Lynda Brody

1a   1b   1c

1a–c: Production images of *PolyMorph*: slip-casting process and final glaze-fired parts.

2: Diagrams highlighting connection combinations and material translation of the generative design strategy based on networking behavior.

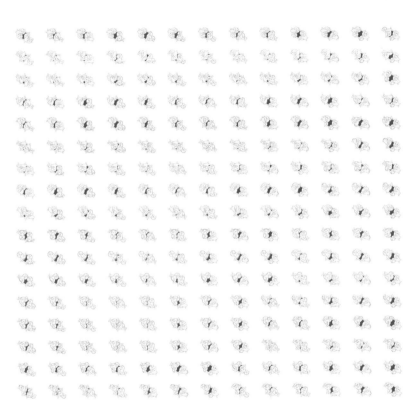

2

3: Drawing of final material assembly. *PolyMorph* is
composed of 1,400 digitally produced and
hand-cast ceramic components interwoven and
tensioned to form a large spatial structure.

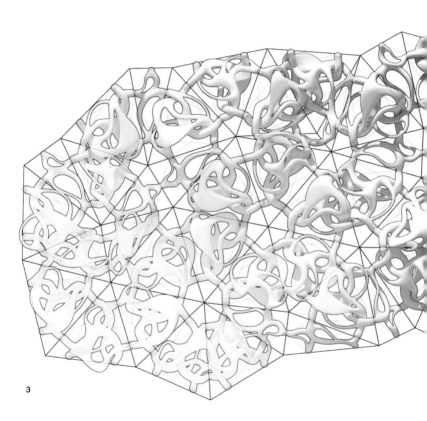

3

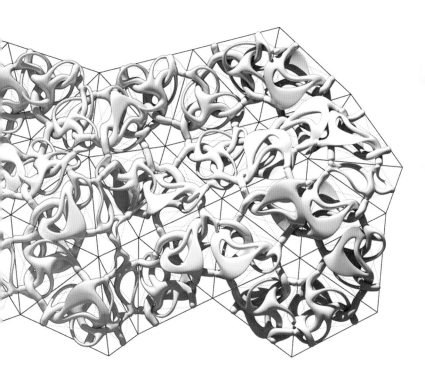

4a–d: Photographs of *PolyMorph* in its final installation

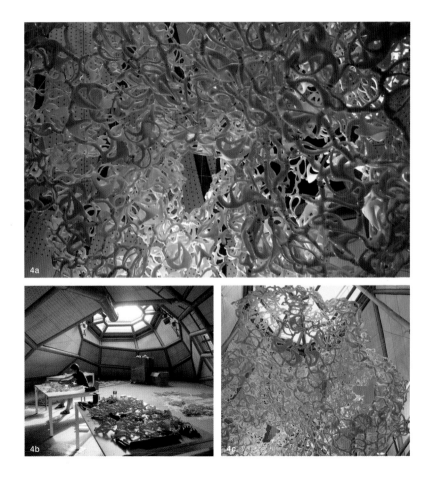

4d

myThread Pavilion

Temporary Pavilion Structure

Nike Stadium, Nike FlyKnit Collective, New York, New York, 2012

The *myThread Pavilion* integrates data from the human body with knitted, lightweight, high-performing, formfitting, and adaptive materials. *myThread* features a generative design strategy that hybridizes the simplicity of knitting processes and fabrication technologies with the flexibility and sensitivity of the human body as a biodynamic model for adaptive forms and fabric architectures.

Can sport, in terms of the measurable performance of the human body, influence both design and fabrication and inspire next-generation materials and structures? What if we could form-fit and enhance architecture with the bioarchitecture and performance of our own bodies? The body, or more specifically the body in motion—pure performance itself—is the starting point of our New York collaboration for this project. Using Nike+ FuelBand technology to collect motion data from a community of runners during an earlier Nike FlyKnit workshop, Jenny Sabin Studio transformed the patterns of this biological data into the geometry and material of knitted structure. Simply put, the generative design strategy is based on prior performances that are translated into present-tense performance through a finely tuned material assembly of knitted threads that respond and adapt to the presence or absence of light. The *myThread Pavilion* is composed of an inner structure of soft, textile-based WHOLEGARMENT knit elements that absorbs, collects, and delivers light as the materials react to variegated light sources and the presence of people through embedded shadows.

The *myThread Pavilion* was commissioned by Nike, Inc. for the International Nike FlyKnit Collective. Jenny Sabin was selected as one of six innovators from around the world to contribute an original work for the collective inspired by the Nike FlyKnit technology and its core benefits. Sabin led the NYC FlyKnit Collective.

Architectural Designer: Jenny E. Sabin; Design and Production Team: James Blair, Simin Wang, Martin Miller, Meagan Whetstone, Brian Heller, Nicola McElroy; Consulting Engineer: Daniel Bosia, AKT Engineers; Consulting Textile Designer: Anne Emlein; Lighting Designer: KayneLive

1a–c: Motion and biological data collection, pattern samples, and knitted material prototypes

2a–c: Knitting simulations and digital models featuring gradients of biological data. These data are linked to changes in material and knitting parameters such as holes and shifts in tension.

3: Construction drawing for placement of
seams between each knitted cone; final drawings
of the Pavilion

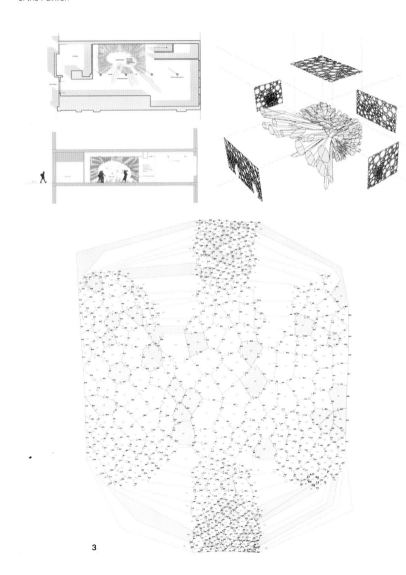

3

4a–d: Day to evening light simulation.
The *myThread Pavilion* features responsive
WHOLEGARMENT-knitted solar active,
photoluminescent, and reflective yarns.

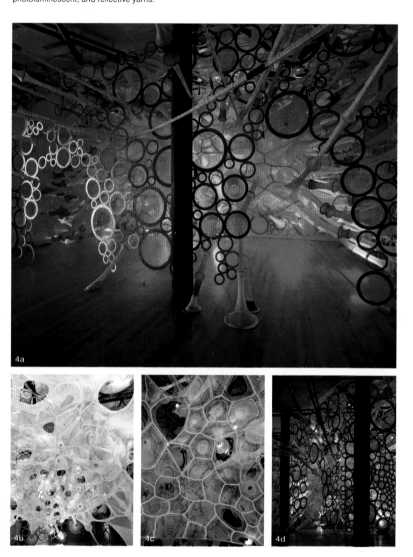

5: Opening night at Nike Stadium, New York.
The interior of the pavilion can comfortably house
thirty people.

5

Geoffrey von Oeyen Design

Geoffrey von Oeyen

Geoffrey von Oeyen Design, founded in Los Angeles, leverages geometric relationships and site conditions to create visual overlays for the spatial registration of place.

Overlay defines the work of the practice, as each project geometrically calibrates one's relationship to site, to views, and to daylight. The following projects mediate between the existing and the new with the aim of reframing and redirecting views, patterns, and orientations. Architectural elements within each project simultaneously serve a multiplicity of functional and aesthetic design objectives that emerge from the complexities of client needs, budget limitations, and site constraints.

These projects are optical devices specifically adapted to represent familiar contexts in unanticipated ways, and are developed through a process that seeks to reveal essential geometric paradigms. Architectural compositions serve alternately as foreground or background, depending on their orientation to the viewer and the viewer's position. Peter Eisenman's trace is reinterpreted in the temporal specificity of place, as Hiroshi Sugimoto's horizons, Donald Judd's voids, and Olafur Eliasson's optics represent the corporeal experience of the natural world. While Rem Koolhaas is correct that we are no longer living in the spatial and moral cosmology of Le Corbusier's *Le poeme de l'angle droit*, the reshaping of our reality in the cultural eddies of modernity requires precisely the sensitivity to site that *junkspace* numbs.

Through new houses, renovations, pavilions, and classrooms, extensions are drawn from contextual buildings and landscapes and then transformed to reframe those contexts. Everyday spaces, in their scale and ubiquity, offer a degree of clarity to the most essential aspects of architecture. Their design reveals the overlay of rituals in daily *praxis*, and the possibilities for those scenarios are embedded in these designs.

The timeliness and timelessness of representing and transforming familiar typologies oblige Geoffrey von Oeyen Design to solve issues of daylight, space, and view not for one-time visitors to be delighted in the singular and novel but as a source of recurring spatial discovery. Complex systems, patterns, and sequences overlaid throughout these seemingly simple spaces are designed to unfold over time. Perspectival alignments, geometric sequences, visual coincidences, shadow projections, daylight diffusion, erosion patterns, and other visual and material phenomena can be understood through an accretion of experiences in and around these buildings, thus revealing the spatial capacities latent in each design.

Overlay
New York, New York, 2014

For the 2014 Architectural League Prize exhibition, two simultaneous problems, site and program, are addressed optically vis-à-vis geometry. The program consists of seventy-three architectural representations by Geoffrey von Oeyen Design, including drawings, renderings, and physical models. The site is the wall of a white box gallery opposite the gallery entry and adjacent to the window facing Fifth Avenue. The program is organized as a field of individual boxes arranged in elevation as a golden rectangle, celebrating and distorting the ubiquity and perceived neutrality of the well-proportioned white-box gallery typology.

The boxes are spatially oriented and obliquely trimmed to the gallery wall to create the metaform of a concave surface that places the standing viewer's eye level at the center. This concave shape is asymmetrically biased in plan to viewers on Fifth Avenue, reflecting daylight and street movements into the gallery. The boxes are locally scaled and angled to program content adjacencies, solid-to-void relationships, and shadow projections. Curved, CNC-cut sides create continuous, canyon-like voids between key programmatic groups, revealing erosion-like traces in the project. The entire installation can be understood as one moment in an animate bas-relief.

1

1: Elevation view
2a–d: Detail views

3: Oblique view toward Fifth Avenue

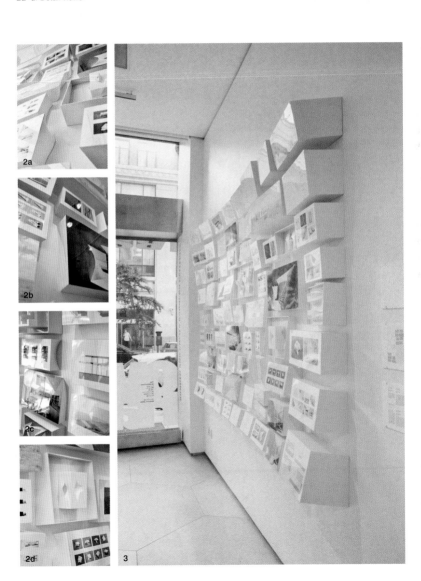

Case Room
Malibu, California, 2013–2014

This major residential addition is a private study for two attorneys working in the north light at the foot of a hillside. Clerestory windows diffuse light, proportion and orient the space, and frame views up the hill. The massing of the Case Room, designed as a series of blocks obliquely sliced and assembled in a descending sequence in section, transitions in plan from a threshold with the existing house to a transposition of the existing exterior wall geometry. Material selections, including vertical timber siding and zinc standing-seam rooms, striate and orient the geometric surfaces. The new second-floor landing adjacent to the Case Room, flanked by an elevator to the west and clerestory light well to the east, frames simultaneous views both into the room and above its roof toward the hillside. The dynamic interplay of reflected light on the ceiling surfaces throughout the day provides gently modulating, diffused top lighting for contemplative work.

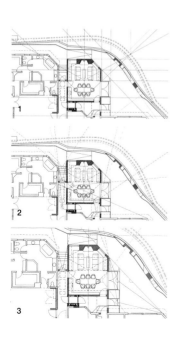

1

2

3

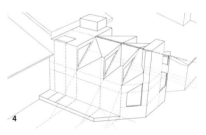

4

5a

5b

1: Parametric geometry overlays
2: Perspective views within
3: Perspective views out
4: Geometric construction of roof planes

5a–b: Exterior massing views
6: Interior view looking north
7: Parametric geometry overlays

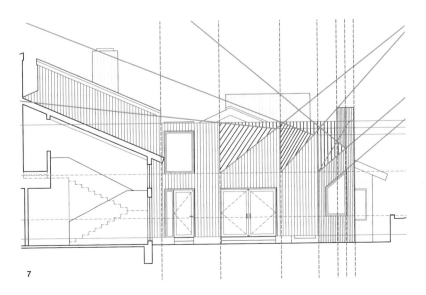

7

8a–e: Model views
9: North elevation with existing house context

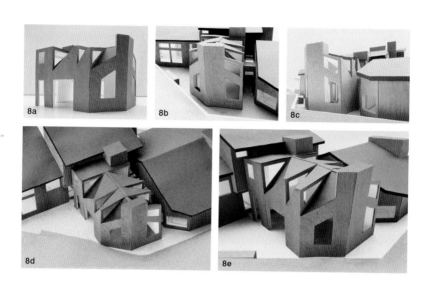

8a
8b
8c
8d
8e

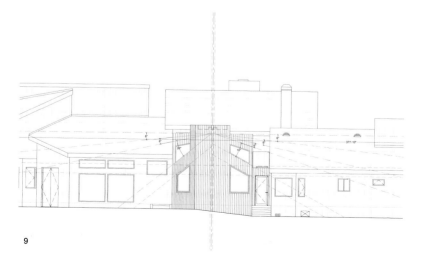

9

10: Sectional daylighting studies
11: Interior view looking south

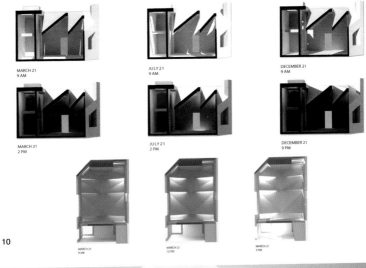

MARCH 21
9 AM

JULY 21
9 AM

DECEMBER 21
9 AM

MARCH 21
2 PM

JULY 21
2 PM

DECEMBER 21
9 PM

10

MARCH 21
9 AM

MARCH 21
12 PM

MARCH 21
3 PM

11

Shadow Box Pavilion
Los Angeles, California, 2013

Referencing Toyo Ito's Serpentine Pavilion and Geoffrey von Oeyen's MPhil research on Le Corbusier's Tower of Shadows as a Fulbright Scholar at the University of Cambridge, this box geometry is overlaid with regulating lines, cut, folded inward, closed, and glazed to reveal the interplay of light and shadow. Geometric cuts follow an overlay of coincident construction lines, and folds in the surfaces invite multiple readings of massing and orientation. Surfaces appear alternately thin and massive or light and heavy, and they appear to prefer space or form depending on vantage point. Place and time are registered by the shadow patterns on the ceiling, walls, and floor. Walls remain plumb from the ground to just above head height, after which they fold inward to reinforce spatial and structural connections. Powder-coated sheet steel to be CNC cut, folded, and welded in position. The folded steel sheets stiffen and reinforce the pavilion's structure, while seams offer positions for glazing frames and sealant.

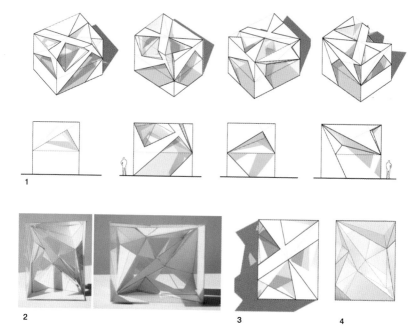

1

2

3

4

1: Oblique views and elevations
2: Ceiling views
3: Roof plan

4: Reflected ceiling plan
5: Oblique views
6: Roof view with shadows

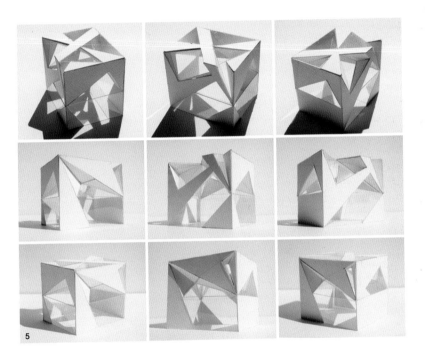

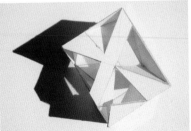

Pool House
Los Angeles, California, 2013

This major residential addition, cut into a steeply sloping canyon hillside, features mirrored L-shaped plans: one that pushes the pool into the hillside and one that projects a double-level cantilevered deck out into the canyon. A continuous retaining wall moves through the house from one side of the site to the other, carving into and pushing out of the hillside to shape light and views, framing the horizon of the Pacific Ocean. The architectural promenade from the main house to the Pool House offers several viewing positions as one descends into the canyon, finally pausing at the roof level. A glazed staircase and skylights penetrate the thick green roof to bring light from above. At the pool-deck level, the ocean view is mirrored in the glazing reflection, visually extending the horizon into the hillside. The project roof is to be constructed using the same formwork and temporary support structures as typical parking garage floors to achieve cost efficiency, while the CMU walls serve as earth retention, pool, and gutter structures.

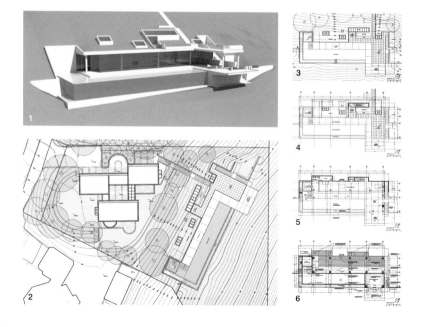

1: View from across the canyon
2: Site plan
3: Roof plan
4: Upper-terrace level
5: Pool-deck level
6: Foundation plan with structural grid overlays

7: Site section overlays indicating daylighting and views
8: Section overlay through upper terrace and cantilevered pool deck
9: Section overlay through pool and interior staircase
10: Perspective view, south

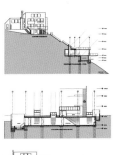

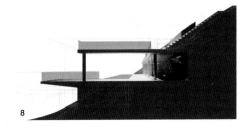

8

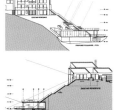

9

10

Horizon House
Malibu, California, 2013–2014

An existing ranch house from the 1960s is to have its ceiling removed and its roof bisected, lifted, and reoriented due south. These new roof planes refocus the view to the Pacific horizon, transforming perspectives outside and within the house. The chamfered addition allows for the pool to be oriented east-west for maximum ocean and daylight exposure along the south-facing Malibu coastline. Following Robin Evans's concept of Mies van der Rohe's paradoxical symmetries in the Barcelona Pavilion, the horizon is mirrored by cantilevered frames supporting operable fabric canopies above and the pool below, which work in concert to overlay diffuse light on the ceiling surfaces. A highly engineered steel-framing system provides for visual and physical extensions outward.

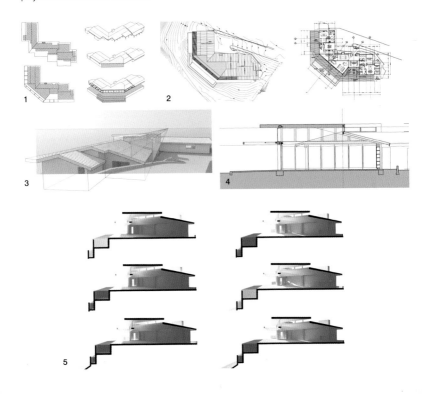

1: New addition overlays

2: New roof and floor plans

3: Perspective overlay of the roofscape as one approaches the house at the top of the driveway; roof and clerestory frame the horizon

4: Existing roof bifurcated, ceiling removed, and new ceiling lifted

5: Sectional daylighting studies

6: Western view across the pool deck

7: New axes reorient key plan relationships

8: Degrees of enclosure and exposure

9: Key views and axes

10: Great room with bifurcated roof and new roof supported by Vierendeel truss systems

Y-House
Marfa, Texas, 2013–2014

The vast expanse of West Texas and proximity to the Chinati Foundation inform the massing and parti of this new retreat for a London family. A covered front courtyard and open rear courtyard provide privacy while shaping expansive views. Subtle plays with siting and perspective are achieved by mirroring the ground topography in the outer roof edge, while the inner rear courtyard roof remains horizontal. The house thus performs differently as an object in the landscape than as an optical device for viewing the landscape. Daylighting is a primary overlay, shaping circulation and programmed spaces. The architectural promenade, beginning with the vehicular approach and including an enfilade arrangement of entry court, living room, and rear courtyard, is an orchestrated sequence that situates this house in the landscape.

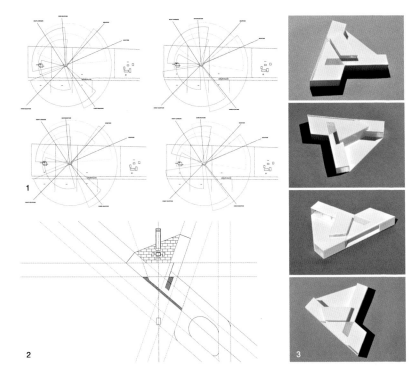

1

2

3

1: Siting and massing strategies per viewshed
2: Site geometry overlays
3a–d: Massing study: 3-D printed model

4: Auto approach: Elevation views
5: Driveway studies
6: View to the west and downtown Marfa

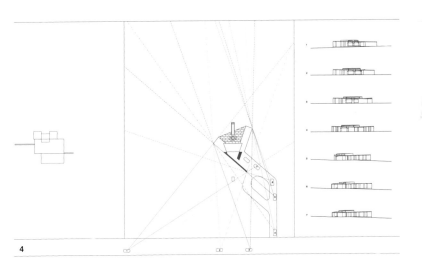

4

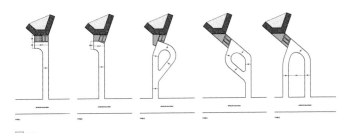

5

6

7: Carport entry lighting studies
8: Parametric courtyard studies
9: View to the southeast

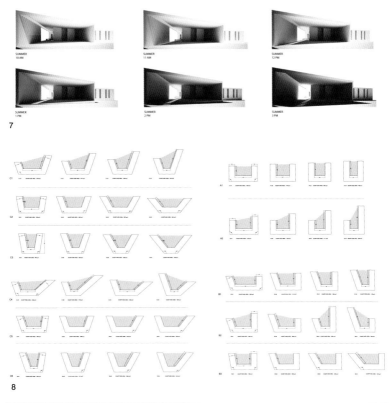

7

8

9

10: Courtyard orientations
11: Symmetrical and asymmetrical alignments about the central axis
12: Viewing sequence: Covered approach to entry

13: View from the road to the north
14: Elevations revealing perspectival distortion as in *La fontaine Médicis*; mirroring above and below the horizon line per the slope contours

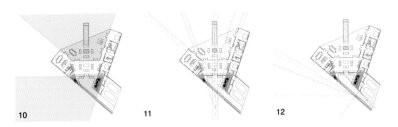

10   11   12

13

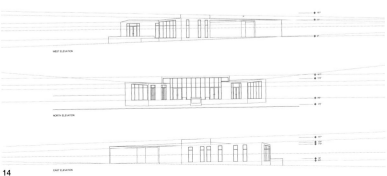

14

15: Entry court daylight studies
16: Entry court view with sloping roof
17: Exterior daylight studies

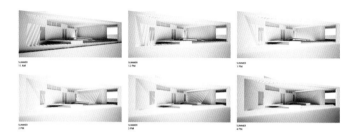

15

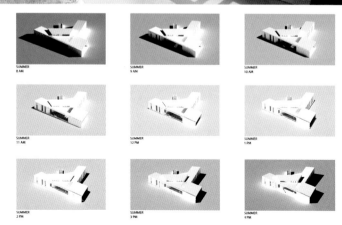

17

18: Entry perspective looking north to the
Davis Mountains
19: Longitudinal section daylighting studies
20: View to the south

SUMMER
12 PM

SUMMER
2 PM

SUMMER
4 PM

WINTER
12 PM

WINTER
2 PM

WINTER
4 PM

19

Project and Idea Realization Lab (PIRL)
Pacific Palisades, California, 2014

PIRL is a new design technology lab and classroom for St. Matthew's Parish School that celebrates the design process as integral to education. Both indoors and out, the two teaching spaces provide comprehensive learning opportunities that enable a critical approach toward multidisciplinary, design-based collaboration. Daylight control and geometric discretization are critical design themes. The student-operated retractable canopy is a didactic expression of architecture, engineering, and sailing design that creates a covered outdoor teaching and making space. The classroom interior, taking spatial and programmatic cues from Stanford's Institute of Design, provides a technology platform for creative collaboration on projects ranging from robotics to filmmaking.

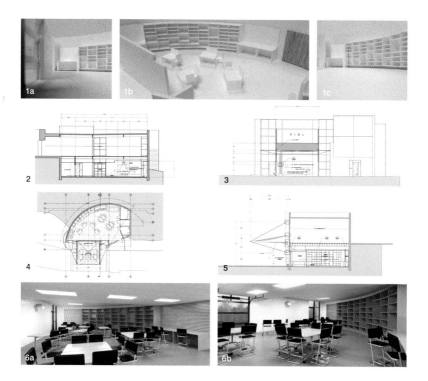

1a–c: Model interior views
2: Section looking to the northeast
3: Exterior elevation
4: First-floor plan

5: Section looking to the southeast
6a–b: 3-D model interior views
7: Closed canopy rendering
8: Open canopy rendering

Casa Dunas

Isabela, Puerto Rico, 2013–2014

This project investigates the building of a house on ecologically sensitive dunes in northwest Puerto Rico for a surfer and landscape architect researching and designing within North Atlantic dune ecologies. The design challenge is to make a project that can be occupied part-time during the year and is capable of being washed through by future ocean storms similar to Hurricane Sandy. Conceptually, the project could be read as being analogous to a seashell for a hermit crab, one that is eroded by waves and wind while cyclically serving as a ruin and a home. The traces of sand-flow patterns through this house inform its design. Overlays of residential form making by John Lautner, the animate forms of Greg Lynn, and architectural precedents in ruled-surface concrete formwork inform the thinking in this project. Curved concrete forms provide greater structural opportunities for resisting wave impacts than plumb walls, as they divert and diffuse the wave forces both vertically and laterally. This design approach allows water and sand to flow over inclined walls, allowing walls to act as anchors to prevent the undermining of the ground floor slab, and, importantly, creates less erosion in the adjacent dunes.

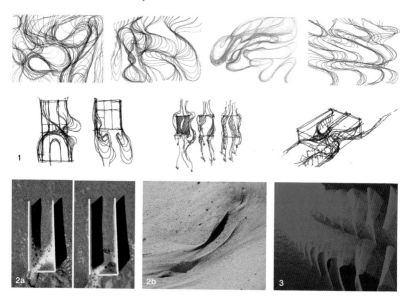

1: Concept sketches: Flow and erosion
pattern studies
2a–b: Erosion patterns and their trace:
Model photographs
3: Animation study: Flow patterns

4: Formal study: Blended shapes
5a–b: Concept design studies
6a–c: 3-D print model views
7: 3-D print model: Flow study

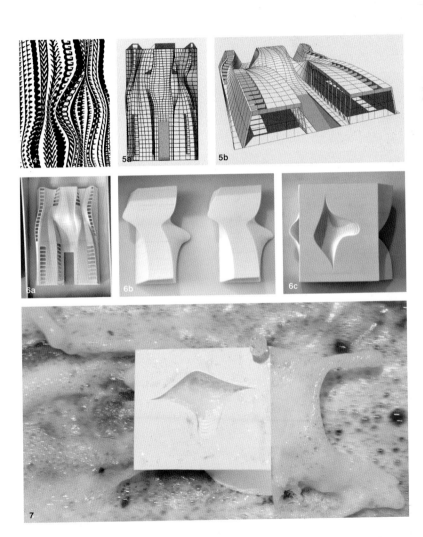

8: 3-D print model: Erosion studies
9: 3-D print model: Erosion study
10: 3-D print model: Detail views

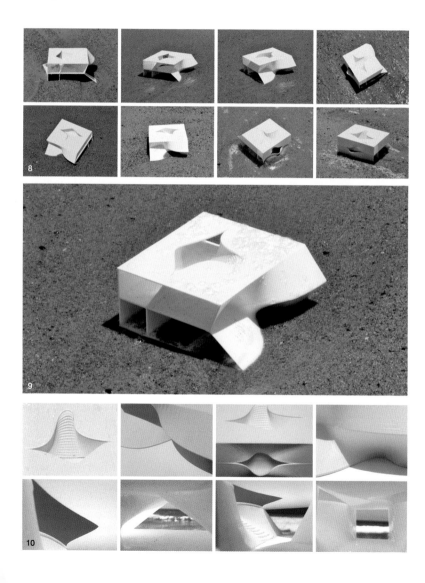

11: 3-D print model: Interior view study
12: Conceptual rendering of interior view

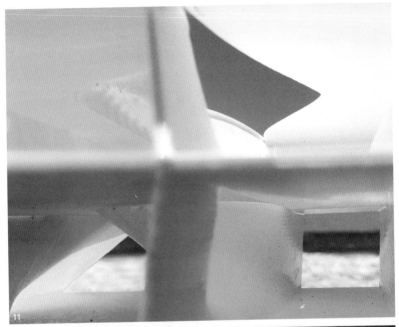